Who Is Jesus?

Exploring the Life, Death, Resurrection, and Teachings of Jesus

Andy Sochor

Who Is Jesus?
Copyright © 2025

All Rights Reserved. No portion of this book may be reproduced in any form without the written permission of the publisher, except in the case of brief excerpts to be used in a review.

Published by:
Gospel Armory Publishing
Bowling Green, Kentucky
www.GospelArmory.com

Printed in the United States of America

ISBN: 978-1-959201-91-5

Table of Contents

Preface   v

Who Is Jesus?   1
Introducing Jesus   2
The Life of Jesus   9
The Death of Jesus   19
The Disciples of Jesus   29

More About Jesus   37
Christ Our Mediator   38
The Shepherd and the Sheep   43
Jesus Christ: Prince of Peace   48
Jesus Christ: Our Perfect Example   53
Jesus: The Great Debater   58
The Way, the Truth, and the Life   65
Another Jesus   67
Testifying of Christ   74
What Was Said About Jesus on the Cross?   81
A Personal Relationship with Jesus   84

Preface

For the past several years, our congregation has been using a four-lesson correspondence course as an outreach tool. The purpose of the course was to concisely teach who Jesus is, discuss His life, explain the significance of His death, and show how we can become His disciples. Since we began using it, people throughout the country and around the world have studied it to help them learn more about Jesus and plant a seed in their hearts that may help them be faithful disciples.

This book contains the four lessons from that course and ten additional articles that provide a more comprehensive picture of Jesus as He is described in the Bible. However, even with the additional articles, this material is just a brief introduction to the Son of God, who came to earth to save us from our sins. We can (and should) spend a lifetime learning more about Jesus and developing a deeper appreciation and reverence for Him.

Whether the material in this short book is new to you or serves as a reminder of what you have already learned, my prayer is that it will spur you on to a deeper study of the Scriptures so that you may grow in faith and knowledge of the Christ.

—Andy Sochor

Who Is Jesus?

Introducing Jesus

"In the beginning was the Word, and the Word was with God, and the Word was God" (John 1:1).

"And the Word became flesh, and dwelt among us, and we saw His glory, glory as of the only begotten from the Father, full of grace and truth" (John 1:14).

The gospel of John was written to teach people about Jesus. The first chapter introduces Jesus to us. We learn of Him through the various words and phrases used to describe the Lord, some of which are found in the verses above. The opening chapter of John is a good place to go to learn, be reminded, or teach others about Jesus. Let us briefly consider some of the ways in which Jesus is described in these verses.

Jesus Is the Word

"In the beginning was the Word..." (John 1:1).

Several points are implied by the word, *Word*. First, the *Word* is an **announcement** – revealing what otherwise would not have been known. Jesus is the spokesman for the Father during these last days (Hebrews 1:2). Jesus said, *"Therefore the things I speak, I speak just as the Father has told Me"* (John 12:50). Second, the *Word* includes **doctrine** – teaching that we must obey. All authority was given to Jesus; therefore, His disciples are to observe His commandments (Matthew 28:18-20). Third, the *Word* indicates a **direction** – a way that we should go. Jesus told His disciples, *"I am the way… no one comes to the Father but through Me"* (John 14:6).

Jesus is not whoever we want Him to be. As the *Word*, He is a divine being with objective standards and expectations of us. We must conform our lives to His will, rather than try to conform Him to our will.

Jesus Is Eternal

"In the beginning was the Word… He was in the beginning with God" (John 1:1-2).

Though Jesus was *"born of a woman"* at a particular time – *"when the fulness of the time came"* (Galatians 4:4) – the Spirit of Christ existed long before that. John the Baptist was born before Jesus (Luke 1:35-36), yet he said of Christ, *"After me comes a Man who has a higher rank than I, for **He existed before me**"* (John 1:30). Jesus said elsewhere, *"Before Abraham was born, I am"* (John 8:58).

Jesus was *"in the beginning with God"* (John 1:2). His existence is eternal, *"having neither beginning of days nor end of life"* (Hebrews 7:3). He was not a created being, but existed *"in the beginning"* – the *"time"* before Creation.

Jesus Is God

"*The Word was God*" (John 1:1).

Jesus was not just a good man, wise teacher, or even a prophet. Jesus was God in the flesh (Matthew 1:23). Isaiah prophesied: "*For a child will be born to us, a son will be given to us; and the government will rest on His shoulders; and His name will be called Wonderful Counselor, Mighty God, Eternal Father, Prince of Peace*" (Isaiah 9:6).

Jesus "*was with God, and...was God*" (John 1:1). He was, and is, one of three persons of the Godhead – the Father (Titus 1:4), the Son (Titus 2:13), and the Holy Spirit (Acts 5:3-4). Jesus was equal with the Father (John 5:18; 10:30) and, while on earth, rightfully accepted worship (Matthew 28:9, 17; Luke 24:52) which is to be directed only to God (Revelation 22:8-9). Jesus was not just a man, but is God.

Jesus Is the Giver of Life

"*All things came into being through Him, and apart from Him nothing came into being that has come into being. In Him was life...*" (John 1:3-4).

John first described Jesus as being the giver of physical life. He was instrumental in Creation (John 1:3). Paul told the brethren in Colossae that Jesus is both the Creator and Sustainer of life. "*For by Him all things were created...all things have been created through Him and for Him. He is before all* things, and in Him all things hold together" (Colossians 1:16-17).

However, Jesus is not just the giver of *physical* life, but also of *spiritual* life. He provides the hope of eternal life for those who are "*born again*" (John 3:3-5, 16). Paul told the saints in Rome, "*For the wages of sin is death, but the free gift of God is eternal life in Christ Jesus our Lord*" (Romans 6:23). Through Jesus, we have the hope of salvation (1 Thessalonians 5:9).

Jesus Is the Light

"*In Him was life, and the life was the Light of men. The Light shines in the darkness, and the darkness did not comprehend it*" (John 1:4-5).

Elsewhere, Jesus said, "*I am the Light of the world; he who follows Me will not walk in the darkness, but will have the Light of life*" (John 8:12). The idea of Jesus being the Light is connected to Him being the Word. The psalmist wrote, "*Your word is a lamp to my feet and a light to my path*" (Psalm 119:105). As the Light, Jesus provides the world with revelation, knowledge, and direction. [We noted these in the first section about Jesus as the Word. He announced what was being revealed, delivered His doctrine which we are to know, and directed us in the path we should go.]

Jesus Became Flesh

"*And the Word became flesh, and dwelt among us...*" (John 1:14).

Jesus becoming flesh was part of God's plan from the beginning. After sin was introduced into the world, God cursed the serpent and revealed a prophecy about the coming of Christ: "*And I will put enmity between you and the woman, and between your seed and her seed; he shall bruise you on the head, and you shall bruise him on the heel*" (Genesis 3:15). Jesus "*partook*" of "*flesh and blood*" so that He could deliver this crushing blow to Satan (Hebrews 2:14). Since "*it is impossible for the blood of bulls and goats to take away sins,*" God prepared "*a body*" for Jesus so that He could make a suitable atonement sacrifice (Hebrews 10:4-5).

However, it is important to note that Jesus "*became flesh*" without surrendering His deity. When the inspired apostle said Jesus "*was God*" (John 1:1), he did not mean that Jesus used to be God but was no longer God. "*Jesus Christ is the same yesterday and today and forever*" (Hebrews 13:8). Paul wrote, "*For in Him all the fullness of Deity dwells in bodily form*" (Colossians 2:9). When Jesus "*became flesh,*" He did not cease to be who He was (God). Instead, His divine spirit inhabited a flesh and blood body.

Jesus Explained the Father

> "*No one has seen God at any time; the only begotten God who is in the bosom of the Father, He has explained Him*" (John 1:18).

In Jesus, the Son of God, we see the Father. Jesus made this clear in a conversation He had with Philip. "*Philip said to Him, 'Lord, show us the Father, and it is enough for us.' Jesus said to him, 'Have I been so long with you, and yet you have not come to know Me, Philip? He who has seen Me has seen the Father; how can you say, "Show us the Father"?"* (John 14:8-9). One can know the Father by examining the works and words of Christ.

This reminds us of Jesus' role in revelation. His works and words show us the Father. "*Therefore Jesus answered and was saying to them, 'Truly, truly, I say to you, the Son can do nothing of Himself, unless it is something He sees the Father doing; for **whatever the Father does, these things the Son also does** in like manner'*" (John 5:19). "*So Jesus said, 'When you lift up the Son of Man, then you will know that I am He, and I do nothing of My own initiative, but **I speak these things as the Father taught Me**'*" (John 8:28). All of this also shows us the unity between the Father and the Son. Jesus said, "*I and the Father are one*" (John 10:30). We cannot accept one and not the other (Luke 10:16).

Jesus Is the Lamb of God

"*The next day he saw Jesus coming to him and said, 'Behold, the Lamb of God who takes away the sin of the world!'*" (John 1:29).

This was Jesus' mission – to make forgiveness available to all men (Luke 24:47; Acts 10:43). He was called a Lamb because He would be sacrificed, just as was done with lambs under the Old Testament system (Exodus 12:3-7; Deuteronomy 16:1-2; 1 Corinthians 5:7). Jesus said, "'*And I, if I am lifted up from the earth, will draw all men to Myself.' But He was saying this to indicate the kind of death by which He was to die*" (John 12:32-33). He came to earth in order to "*give*

His life a ransom for many" (Matthew 20:28). Forgiveness is available "*through His blood*" which He shed on the cross (Ephesians 1:7).

Jesus' death on the cross was not for His own sins – He had none (Isaiah 53:9; 1 Peter 2:22). Instead of dying for His sins, He made atonement for our sins (Romans 5:8-11). However, if we want to be saved from our sins, we must take advantage of His sacrifice. That means obeying Him (Hebrews 5:9) – this includes baptism in which our sins are washed away (Acts 2:38; 22:16) – and remaining faithful until death (Revelation 2:10).

Conclusion

The first chapter of John is a great place to go to be reminded about Jesus – who He is and what He came to do. It is also a good place to go to teach people who are not familiar with Jesus. Let us remember the lessons contained in this chapter so that we might faithfully follow Him and try to bring others to Him as well.

The Life of Jesus

"*And the Word became flesh, and dwelt among us*" (John 1:14). In this statement, John was referring to Jesus who came to earth to live among men. This was necessary in order to fulfill His mission through His death on the cross (Hebrews 2:14). We will examine the death of Jesus in more detail in a future article. In this article, we are going to take a broad look at the life of Jesus and see what we can learn and apply to our lives.

His Birth

In Luke's account of the birth of Jesus, notice how he recorded it as a historical event:

> "*Now in those days a decree went out from Caesar Augustus, that a census be taken of all the inhabited earth. This was the first census taken while Quirinius was governor of Syria. And everyone was on his way to register for the census, each to his own city.*
>
> "*Joseph also went up from Galilee, from the city of Nazareth, to Judea, to the city of David*

> which is called Bethlehem, because he was of the house and family of David, in order to register along with Mary, who was engaged to him, and was with child. While they were there, the days were completed for her to give birth. And she gave birth to her firstborn son; and she wrapped Him in cloths, and laid Him in a manger, because there was no room for them in the inn" (Luke 2:1-7).

Luke did not use vague or generic terms in describing the setting of Jesus' birth as if it were merely a legend or myth. Instead, he identified the time it occurred, who was ruling at time, and what the circumstances were that led to Jesus being born in Bethlehem.

Jesus' birth was also announced by angels. Angels are God's messengers (Acts 7:53). In fact, the Greek word is the same for both angels and messengers (*angelos*). The angel Gabriel told Mary of Jesus and her role in bringing Him into the world (Luke 1:26-33). After His birth, angels appeared and praised God to announce His coming (Luke 2:13-14). The fact that angels – who were God's messengers – announced His birth indicates that it was part of God's plan.

Jesus' birth was also the fulfillment of prophecy. Notice just a couple of these prophecies:

> *"Therefore the Lord Himself will give you a sign: Behold, a virgin will be with child and bear a son, and she will call His name Immanuel"* (Isaiah 7:14).

"But as for you, Bethlehem Ephrathah, too little to be among the clans of Judah, from you One will go forth for Me to be ruler in Israel. His goings forth are from long ago, from the days of eternity" (Micah 5:2).

In the first prophecy, Isaiah indicated that the Messiah would be born of a virgin – something that was not naturally possible. When the angel announced to Mary that should would *"conceive in [her] womb and bear a son,"* she asked how it was possible since she was *"a virgin"* (Luke 1:31, 34). The angel explained, *"The Holy Spirit will come upon you, and the power of the Most High will overshadow you; and for that reason the holy Child shall be called the Son of God"* (Luke 1:35).

In the second prophecy, Bethlehem was identified as the place where the Messiah would be born. Luke recorded that Joseph and Mary traveled to Bethlehem for the census and it was there that Jesus was born (Luke 2:4-7).

These are just two examples, but they show that God knew and, therefore, was able to reveal these details hundreds of years before they happened. These could not have been mere guesses. They had to have come from God.

His Childhood

The gospels only record one event from Jesus' childhood – the time when He was twelve years old and His family lost Him and found Him later in the temple (Luke 2:41-52). Let us notice a few verses from this occasion:

> "Then, after three days they found Him in the temple, sitting in the midst of the teachers, both listening to them and asking them questions. And all who heard Him were amazed at His understanding and His answers.
>
> "When they saw Him, they were astonished; and His mother said to Him, 'Son, why have You treated us this way? Behold, Your father and I have been anxiously looking for You.' And He said to them, 'Why is it that you were looking for Me? Did you not know that I had to be in My Father's house?' But they did not understand the statement which He had made to them.
>
> "And He went down with them and came to Nazareth, and He continued in subjection to them; and His mother treasured all these things in her heart. And Jesus kept increasing in wisdom and stature, and in favor with God and men" (Luke 2:46-52).

There are some important lessons we can learn from this one event. First, Jesus knew where He came from. He "*had to be in* [His] *Father's house*" (Luke 2:49). He was more than just "*the carpenter's son*" (Matthew 13:55); He was the Son of God. The teachers of the law "*were amazed at His understanding*" (Luke 2:47). He was too young to be highly educated, yet He was. Later the leaders were "*astonished*" because He had "*become learned, having never been educated*" (John 7:15). Of course, He was certainly not *uneducated*. While He had no formal education, He received His teaching from the one who sent Him (John 7:16) – the Father.

Second, while on earth Jesus was still God in the flesh. It is significant that He referred to the Father as *"My Father"* (Luke 2:49). This indicated *equality* with the Father. The Jews understood this later when He referred to the Father this way: *"But He answered them, 'My Father is working until now, and I Myself am working.' For this reason therefore the Jews were seeking all the more to kill Him, because He…was calling God His own Father, making Himself equal with God"* (John 5:17-18). Paul wrote that while Jesus was on the earth that *"all the fullness of Deity* [dwelled] *in bodily form"* (Colossians 2:9). He was still God while He was living in the flesh.

Third, as a child Jesus submitted to His earthly parents. After they found Him in the temple *"He went down with them and came to Nazareth, and He continued in subjection to them"* (Luke 2:51). This was what the Law of Moses required (Exodus 20:12). In obeying this command, Jesus set an example for all children to follow – to *"obey* [their] *parents in the Lord"* (Ephesians 6:1).

Fourth, Jesus grew in different areas. He *"kept increasing in wisdom and stature, and in favor with God and men"* (Luke 2:52). Notice each of these areas:

- **Wisdom** – It is significant that He grew in *wisdom* and not in *knowledge*. Since He was God in the flesh and God is omniscient (Psalm 147:5), He could not have grown in knowledge. However, wisdom is the application of knowledge. As Jesus

grew, He would enter various stages in life that would bring certain responsibilities and expectations. The fact that He grew in wisdom means that He practiced what was right in every stage of life.
- **Stature** – Jesus had a regular, human, flesh and blood body. This was the type of body that the Father "*prepared for* [Him]" to fulfill His mission on earth (Hebrews 10:5).
- **Favor with God** – This was done by pleasing the Father *[more on this in a moment]*.
- **Favor with men** – This was done by fulfilling the Law perfectly. In doing this, He demonstrated love since "*love is the fulfillment of the law*" (Romans 13:10). Therefore, by acting in this way, He would have gained the favor of others.

Fulfilling the Father's Will

Jesus' purpose in coming to earth was to do the Father's will (Hebrews 10:9). This would include His sacrifice on the cross (Hebrews 10:10). As Paul wrote, Jesus was "*obedient to the point of death, even death on a cross*" (Philippians 2:8).

However, the fact that Jesus *obeyed* the Father and submitted to the Father's will did not mean that there was a conflict between Jesus' will and the Father's will. They were in perfect agreement with one another. Jesus made this clear when He said, "*And He who sent Me is with Me; He has not left Me alone, for I always do the things that are pleasing to Him*" (John 8:29). Later He said succinctly, "*I and the Father are one*" (John 10:30).

There is one *alleged* example of conflict between the wills of the Father and the Son in Jesus' prayer in the Garden before His crucifixion: *"My Father, if it is possible, let this cup pass from Me; yet not as I will, but as You will"* (Matthew 26:39). Some believe that Jesus' will at this time was to avoid the cross, putting His will at odds with the Father's will. Yet a closer examination of the passage indicates that this was not a conflict at all. The *"cup"* that Jesus prayed to be removed was the *hour*, not the *cross* (Mark 14:35). He was not praying to *abort* the mission, but for help to *complete* His mission. This prayer was answered (Luke 22:43). The Father and the Son were always united in perfect agreement with one another. There was never any conflict between them.

Jesus perfectly fulfilled the Father's will. Before His arrest, He prayed, *"I glorified You on the earth, having accomplished the work which You have given Me to do"* (John 17:4). He glorified the Father by doing the will of the Father. He did this by fulfilling the Law (Matthew 5:17), testifying to the truth (John 18:37), and willingly laying down His life on the cross (John 10:17-18).

Leaving Us a Perfect Example

Jesus lived a life without sin. Peter wrote that Jesus *"committed no sin, nor was any deceit found in His mouth"* (1 Peter 2:22). This was necessary in order to make His sacrifice on the cross *[more on this in the next article]*. However, His sinless life was also an example for us. In the previous verse, Peter wrote, *"For you have been called for this purpose, since Christ also suffered for you, leaving you an example for you to follow in His steps"* (1 Peter 2:21). We are to live as Jesus lived.

This means that it does matter to God how we live our lives. Jesus will save those who obey Him (Hebrews 5:9). Once we begin following Him, He does not want us to continue in sin. John indicated that his letter was written so that Christians *"may not sin"* (1 John 2:1). On at least two occasions during His earthly ministry, Jesus instructed people to cease from sin (John 5:14; 8:11).

Therefore, we must strive to overcome sin in our lives. Paul made this clear in his letter to the Romans. He responded to their attitude that they could *"continue in sin so that grace may increase"* by saying, *"May it never be! How shall we who died to sin still live in it?"* (Romans 6:1-2). He went on to describe the fact that *"our old self was crucified with Him, in order that our body of sin might be done away with, so that we would no longer be slaves to sin; for he who has died is freed from sin"* (Romans 6:6-7). As Christians, we are to *"consider* [ourselves] *to be dead to sin, but alive to God in Christ Jesus"* (Romans 6:11). We are *"not* [to] *let sin reign in* [our] *mortal body"* or use our bodies as *"instruments of unrighteousness"* (Romans 6:12-13).

Jesus showed us how to overcome temptation when He was tempted by the devil (Matthew 4:1-11). Notice what He taught us about overcoming temptation on that occasion:

- **Remember the word** – Each time Jesus was tempted, He began His response by saying, *"It is written…"* (Matthew 4:4, 7, 10). He used the word of God to overcome temptation. We must remember God's word so it can also help us overcome the temptations that we face.

- **Remember that God's word means what He intended** – In one of the temptations, the devil quoted Scripture in an attempt to convince Jesus to throw Himself down from the pinnacle of the temple (Matthew 4:5-6; cf. Psalm 91:11-12). However, the devil pulled that passage out of context. When that passage was given by inspiration, it was not God's intention for it to be used to make the point that the devil tried to make with it. That is why Jesus said, "*On the other hand, it is written, 'You shall not put the Lord your God to the test'*" (Matthew 4:7). Context is important. We need to be sure that we are using the Scriptures in the way that God intended, rather than twisting them to justify what the devil is tempting us to do.
- **Remember God's promises** – The devil promised to give Jesus "*all the kingdoms of the world*" if He would "*fall down and worship*" him (Matthew 4:8-9). However, even if the devil could deliver on that promise, Jesus was already going to receive something far better. He would have "*a kingdom which will never be destroyed, and that kingdom will not be left for another people; it will crush and put an end to all these kingdoms, but it will itself endure forever*" (Daniel 2:44). Even if the devil could give Jesus what he promised Him, it paled in comparison with what the Father was going to give to Jesus. The same is true today with the promises that God has made to us – whatever Satan offers us cannot compare with what God has promised us.
- **Remember the temporary nature of earthly things** – Whatever the devil promises is of a tem-

poral nature. Jesus said, "*Do not store up for yourselves treasures on earth, where moth and rust destroy, and where thieves break in and steal*" (Matthew 6:19). Peter said, "*But the day of the Lord will come like a thief, in which the heavens will pass away with a roar and the elements will be destroyed with intense heat, and the earth and its works will be burned up*" (2 Peter 3:10). One day, everything of this life will be destroyed. All that will remain will be those things that are of a spiritual nature.

We must follow Jesus' example and live in such a way that we can say that "*Christ lives in* [us]" (Galatians 2:20).

Conclusion

As we go through life, we must remember the life of Jesus. Let us follow His example of obedience, regardless of the consequences.

The Death of Jesus

"In the beginning was the Word, and the Word was with God, and the Word was God" (John 1:1).

"And the Word became flesh, and dwelt among us, and we saw His glory, glory as of the only begotten from the Father, full of grace and truth" (John 1:14).

In the previous article, we considered the life of Jesus. He perfectly fulfilled the Father's will – even in His death. This article will focus on the death of Jesus and what we should understand about it.

God's Plan

When Peter preached the first gospel sermon on the day of Pentecost, he said that Jesus' death on the cross was part of the *"predetermined plan and foreknowledge of God"* (Acts 2:23). Jesus was described as *"the Lamb slain from the foundation of the world"* (Revelation 13:8, KJV). The Father knew that Jesus would suffer the death that He did on the cross.

Because He knew about this, there were many prophecies given to men that foretold of Jesus' death. Regarding prophecies, Peter wrote, "*But know this first of all, that no prophecy of Scripture is a matter of one's own interpretation, for no prophecy was ever made by an act of human will, but men moved by the Holy Spirit spoke from God*" (2 Peter 1:20-21). In other words, the prophecies about Jesus and His death came directly from God through the Holy Spirit. Notice just a few of these prophecies:

> "*And I will put enmity between you* [the serpent, as] *and the woman, and between your seed and her seed; He* [Jesus, as] *shall bruise you on the head, and you shall bruise him on the heel*" (Genesis 3:15).
>
> "*For dogs have surrounded me; a band of evildoers has encompassed me; they pierced my hands and my feet. I can count all my bones. They look, they stare at me; they divide my garments among them, and for my clothing they cast lots*" (Psalm 22:16-18; cf. John 20:25; Matthew 27:35).
>
> "*But He was pierced through for our transgressions, He was crushed for our iniquities; the chastening for our well-being fell upon Him, and by His scourging we are healed*" (Isaiah 53:5; cf. Matthew 27:26).

This means that Jesus' death on the cross was not an unexpected development. God *knew* it would happen and announced it on multiple occasions centuries before it took place. This is important in light of the popular theory of *premillennialism*.

What is *premillennialism*? This is the theory that Jesus will return one day, set up His kingdom on the earth, and then reign for a thousand years. According to this theory, the reason why it is necessary for Jesus to return to do this is because He failed to set up His kingdom the first time He came since the people rejected Him.

However, Jesus did *not* fail in His mission. He told the Father that He *"accomplished the work"* He had been given to do (John 17:4). If Jesus' mission was to establish an earthly kingdom, He would have done it. On one occasion He had five thousand men ready to *"take Him by force and make Him king"* (John 6:15). Even if He did not have these, He had the authority to call down *"more than twelve legions of angels"* to stop His crucifixion (Matthew 26:53). But He had to die on the cross so that *"the Scriptures* [could] *be fulfilled"* (Matthew 26:54). The theory of *premillennialism* completely misses the point of Jesus' mission.

We are not waiting for a future kingdom. We can be part of the kingdom now. Paul told the brethren in Colossae, *"For He rescued us from the domain of darkness, and transferred us to the kingdom of His beloved Son"* (Colossians 1:13). They were not waiting for the Lord to establish His kingdom at some point in the future. They were already in the kingdom! That means that we can also be in the Lord's kingdom now. This is because the kingdom is the church (Matthew 16:18-19) and it was established on the day of Pentecost following Jesus' death on the cross (Mark 9:1; Acts 1:8; 2:1-4, 47).

All of this is to say that Jesus' death on the cross was part of God's plan from the beginning. He made that clear in His word.

Jesus' Willing Sacrifice

Jesus described Himself as "*the good shepherd* [who] *lays down His life for the sheep*" (John 10:11). He contrasted Himself with the "*hired hand*" who was "*not concerned about the sheep*" and fled whenever danger came (John 10:12-13). Jesus was concerned about the sheep, not just Himself. Because of this, Paul used Jesus as the perfect example of humility and sacrifice:

> "*Have this attitude in yourselves which was also in Christ Jesus, who, although He existed in the form of God, did not regard equality with God a thing to be grasped, but emptied Himself, taking the form of a bond-servant, and being made in the likeness of men. Being found in appearance as a man, He humbled Himself by becoming obedient to the point of death, even death on a cross*" (Philippians 2:5-8).

Jesus put the needs of mankind ahead of His own. Rather than saving Himself from the cross, He suffered and died on the cross so that He could save us. Furthermore, He *willingly* did this. Jesus said, "*For this reason the Father loves Me, be-*

cause I lay down My life so that I may take it again. No one has taken it away from Me, but I lay it down on My own initiative" (John 10:17-18).

Remember that Jesus' death was part of God's "*predetermined plan*" (Acts 2:23). This means that Jesus knew the reason why He came to earth – that He would die on the cross. In fact, He even foretold what would happen. Notice a couple of examples:

> "*From that time Jesus began to show His disciples that He must go to Jerusalem, and suffer many things from the elders and chief priests and scribes, and be killed, and be raised up on the third day*" (Matthew 16:21).
>
> "'*And I, if I am lifted up from the earth, will draw all men to Myself.' But He was saying this to indicate the kind of death by which He was to die*" (John 12:32-33).

Jesus knew what would happen to Him and yet He did not desire to escape the cross [*this point is discussed more in the previous article*]. If He did desire to save Himself from the cross, He would have (Matthew 26:53). Yet He willingly laid down His life for us (John 10:17-18).

Made Forgiveness Possible

When Jesus instituted the Lord's Supper, His explanation of what the cup represented indicated the reason why His blood would be shed: "*And when He had taken a cup and giv-*

en thanks, He gave it to them, saying, 'Drink from it, all of you; for this is My blood of the covenant, which is poured out for many for forgiveness of sins"* (Matthew 26:27-28). Paul said that *"we have redemption through His blood, the forgiveness of our trespasses"* (Ephesians 1:7).

The sacrifices that were offered under the old law tied forgiveness to the shedding of blood. Regarding the sacrifices offered on the day of atonement, the Lord said, *"For the life of the flesh is in the blood, and I have given it to you on the altar to make atonement for your souls; for it is the blood by reason of the life that makes atonement"* (Leviticus 17:11). The Hebrew writer pointed out this connection between the shedding of blood and forgiveness: *"And according to the Law, one may almost say, all things are cleansed with blood, and without shedding of blood there is no forgiveness"* (Hebrews 9:22). The sacrifices that were offered under the Law of Moses could not take away sin (Hebrews 10:4), but they foreshadowed the sacrifice of Christ. Because the shedding of His blood makes forgiveness possible, Jesus' death is part of the foundation of the gospel (1 Corinthians 15:3).

On this point, it is important that we understand that Jesus' sacrifice makes forgiveness *possible* for us *if* we will meet the conditions of pardon that He has given. Many in the religious world believe that we are saved unconditionally, but this is not the case. Jesus is *"to all those who obey Him the source of eternal salvation"* (Hebrews 5:9). Jesus explained the conditional nature of forgiveness when He gave the Great Commission: *"He who has believed and has been baptized shall be saved; but he who has disbelieved shall be condemned"* (Mark 16:16).

Many believe that Jesus only died for the "elect," but this is also not true. Jesus indicated that His death was for *all mankind* when He said, "*For God so loved the world, that He gave His only begotten Son, that whoever believes in Him shall not perish, but have eternal life*" (John 3:16). Paul wrote, "*For the grace of God has appeared, bringing salvation to all men*" (Titus 2:11). This means that salvation is open to *everyone*, as long as they will conform to Jesus' death, burial, and resurrection. Paul explained this in his letter to Rome:

"*Or do you not know that all of us who have been baptized into Christ Jesus have been baptized into His death? Therefore we have been buried with Him through baptism into death, so that as Christ was raised from the dead through the glory of the Father, so we too might walk in newness of life*" (Romans 6:3-4).

"*But thanks be to God that though you were slaves of sin, you became obedient from the heart to that form of teaching to which you were committed, and having been freed from sin, you became slaves of righteousness*" (Romans 6:17-18).

If we will do what the Scriptures say we must do to be saved, we can be forgiven of our sins by the blood of Jesus.

There is a question about the nature of Jesus' sacrifice on the cross. Was it an *atonement* sacrifice or a *substitution* (that He died in our place or in our stead)? What do these mean?

- If Jesus' sacrifice was a *substitutionary* (vicarious) death, then Jesus would have suffered the punishment that was due us (dying in our place). Therefore, we would be free from punishment. However, Jesus did *not* suffer the punishment that was due us. This punishment is *spiritual* death (Romans 6:23), ending in *"the lake of fire* [which] *is the second death"* (Revelation 20:14). This did not happen to Jesus (Psalm 22:24; John 8:29; Luke 23:43). But if Jesus died as our *substitute* and received the punishment that we were due for our sins, then we could not be lost. This would mean that the Calvinistic doctrines of unconditional election, irresistible grace, and the perseverance of the saints would be correct. Yet this is not what the Scriptures teach.
- If Jesus' death was an *atonement* sacrifice, that means His sacrifice delayed God's wrath against us, giving us time to repent and be forgiven. This is illustrated in the example of the plague that God sent against the children of Israel following the punishment of Korah, Dathan, and Abiram. After the plague began moving through the congregation, Aaron *"ran into the midst of the assembly [and] put on the incense and made atonement for the people. He took his stand between the dead and the living, so that the plague was checked"* (Numbers 16:47-48). These people would still eventually be punished by God as they died in the wilderness, but His wrath was turned away at this time and delayed against them. Jesus' sacrifice made atonement for us in the same way. God's wrath still ex-

ists (2 Thessalonians 1:7-9; Romans 2:4-6), but because of His sacrifice we have time to repent and avoid punishment for our sins if we will meet His conditions.

As the Hebrew writer said, "*Without shedding of blood there is no forgiveness*" (Hebrews 9:22). Without Jesus' blood being shed on the cross in His death, we would have no hope.

The Resurrection

When we consider the death of Jesus, we also need to remember His resurrection. Jesus did not just die on the cross. He was also raised from the dead. The angels who met the women at His tomb said, "*Why do you seek the living One among the dead? He is not here, but He has risen. Remember how He spoke to you while He was still in Galilee*" (Luke 24:5-6).

Paul described Jesus as "*the firstborn from the dead*" (Colossians 1:18). This does not mean He was the first one to be raised from the dead – there were others recorded in the Bible who had been raised from the dead before Jesus. Instead, this means that Jesus was the first to be raised to *never die again*. Paul wrote, "*Knowing that Christ, having been raised from the dead, is never to die again; death no longer is master over Him*" (Romans 6:9). He defeated Satan and his power over death. The Hebrew writer pointed this out:

> "*Therefore since the children share in flesh and blood, He Himself likewise also partook of the same, that through death He might render*

> *powerless him who had the power of death, that is, the devil, and might free those who through fear of death were subject to slavery all their lives*" (Hebrews 2:14-15).

Furthermore, the resurrection was a *historical fact*, not a myth. This can be seen in the fact that there were hundreds of eyewitnesses to Jesus' resurrection (1 Corinthians 15:4-8). It can also be seen in the lives of the apostles who went from a state of *fear* (John 20:19) to being willing to die for their testimony (Acts 5:28-29, 40-42). If they knew what they said about the resurrection of Jesus was a lie, they had no reason to suffer as they did (1 Corinthians 15:32). The only reasonable explanation as to why all of them were willing to suffer to the point of death was that they *knew* their message of Jesus being raised from the dead was undeniably *true*.

We have hope through the resurrection of Jesus. Paul wrote, "*But now Christ has been raised from the dead, the first fruits of those who are asleep*" (1 Corinthians 15:20). This means that as Christ was raised, we have hope of also being raised. Peter wrote that we have "*a living hope through the resurrection of Jesus Christ from the dead*" (1 Peter 1:3). We are "*reconciled to God through the death of His Son*" and "*saved by His life*" (Romans 5:10).

Conclusion

Jesus died to save us, but we must take advantage of His sacrifice. This means we must obey the gospel and then live as servants of righteousness (Romans 6:3-4, 17-18).

The Disciples of Jesus

We are now going to consider what the Bible has to say about the disciples of Jesus. The word disciple means a learner or pupil and implies that one is following a master/teacher. The gospel calls us to be disciples of Jesus and shows us the blessings that come from being one of His disciples.

The Charge to Make Disciples

When Jesus gave the Great Commission, He told His apostles to *"make disciples"* (Matthew 28:19). But how would this be done? Notice two accounts of the Great Commission:

> *"And Jesus came up and spoke to them, saying, 'All authority has been given to Me in heaven and on earth. Go therefore and make disciples of all the nations, baptizing them in the name of the Father and the Son and the Holy Spirit, teaching them to observe all that I commanded you...'"* (Matthew 28:18-20).

> *"And He said to them, 'Go into all the world and preach the gospel to all creation. He who has believed and has been baptized shall be*

> *saved; but he who has disbelieved shall be condemned'"* (Mark 16:15-16).

How would Jesus' apostles *"make disciples"*? It would be done through preaching (Mark 16:15), baptizing (Mark 16:16; Matthew 28:19), and teaching the need for continued obedience (Matthew 28:20). But the foundation for all of this was the authority of Christ (Matthew 28:18). Without this, there would be no reason for people to listen to or obey the gospel.

Jesus made the same point when He spoke of those who were *"truly* [His] *disciples"* (John 8:31). But rather than specifying *authority* as the foundation of discipleship, He discussed His *deity* in that context. Deity necessarily implies *authority.* Just a little bit earlier, Jesus taught that believing in His deity was essential for salvation.

> *"Therefore I said to you that you will die in your sins; for unless you believe that I am He, you will die in your sins"* (John 8:24).

The word *"He"* in that verse was added by the translators.* Your Bible may have the word in italics to indicate this. What Jesus was actually saying was this: *"Unless you believe that **I Am**, you will die in your sins."* This is a clear reference to the name of God – the *"I AM"* – as He called Moses to lead the people out of Egypt (Exodus 3:14). By calling Himself, *"I Am,"* Jesus was claiming to be God. The Jews understood this and wanted to stone Him to death for saying it

---

* This does not mean the translations are *wrong.* But it does help us to interpret the passage properly if we understand this.

(John 8:56-59). But this is the foundation for discipleship. We must believe that Jesus was not just a man, but that He was God in the flesh (Colossians 2:9).

Many people in the religious world believe that Jesus is the Son of God. Does this make them *truly* His disciples? Not necessarily. It is the starting point, but not the end.

The Mark of True Disciples

When Jesus taught on this occasion, John recorded that "*many came to believe in Him*" (John 8:30). His comments about discipleship were directed to "*those Jews who had believed Him*" (John 8:31).

Jesus explained that true discipleship was *conditional*. He indicated the conditional nature of discipleship by making an "if/then" statement: "***If** you continue in My word, **then** you are truly disciples of Mine*" (John 8:31). The condition for discipleship was *continuing in His word*.

This condition makes sense. After all, a disciple is a *learner*. Therefore, it is apparent that if we are to be *disciples* of Christ, we must *learn* and continue in His word. Remember the Great Commission to "*make disciples.*" How would one become and remain a disciple?

- One would be *taught* the gospel (Mark 16:15).
- One would *believe* the gospel (Mark 16:16).
- One would *obey* the gospel – namely in baptism (Mark 16:16; Matthew 28:19).
- One would *continue in obedience* (Matthew 28:20).

One might believe in what he has been told about Christ or what he thinks about Christ. But if he does not hear, believe, and obey the gospel, he is not a disciple.

The Blessings of Discipleship

Jesus, because of who He is, could simply demand obedience without any positive incentive. Yet He blesses those who follow Him. The Hebrew writer said, *"And without faith it is impossible to please Him, for he who comes to God must believe that He is and that He is a rewarder of those who seek Him"* (Hebrews 11:6). What are the rewards of seeking after Him? Jesus explained it in the passage above (John 8:31-36).

First, those who are Jesus' disciples will *"know the truth"* (John 8:32). From our perspective, this point may seem obvious. A disciple continues in His word; His word is truth (John 17:17). However, this would not have been the immediate conclusion to Jesus' original audience. In this statement, He made it clear to them that He was speaking the truth from God (John 8:26, 28). By continuing in His word, they would *"know the truth."* The same is true for us today.

Second, those who are Jesus' disciples, since they *"know the truth,"* they have the promise that *"the truth will make [them] free"* (John 8:32). In what sense does the truth make us free? It makes us free from sin. In responding to His audience's objection to the idea that they needed to be freed from anything, Jesus said, *"Truly, truly, I say to you, everyone who commits sin is the slave of sin"* (John 8:34). We must give up sin, not continue to live in it (Romans 6:1-7). After being *"freed from sin,"* we must become *"slaves of righteousness"* (Romans 6:18).

Third, those who are truly the Lord's disciples will be saved. This is the point of Jesus' statement about being made free from being a *"slave of sin"* (John 8:34). Though it is not explicitly stated in the text, it is implied in Jesus' statement. Sin separates us from God (Isaiah 59:2). Being freed from sin, we can be reconciled to God (Ephesians 2:16). Salvation is for *"all those who obey Him"* (Hebrews 5:9). Punishment is for those who do not (2 Thessalonians 1:8-9).

How to Become a Disciple

How does one become a disciple? To answer this question, we can look at the instructions the Lord and His apostles gave to those who would be His followers. Looking to the New Testament, we can see that in order to become a disciple, an individual must:

- **Hear the gospel** – *"And He said to them, 'Go into all the world and preach the gospel to all creation'"* (Mark 16:15). The gospel must be preached because people must hear it in order to respond to it. Jesus said, *"He who has ears to hear, let him hear"* (Luke 8:8).
- **Believe that Jesus is the Christ** – *"He who has believed and has been baptized shall be saved; but he who has disbelieved shall be condemned"* (Mark 16:16). Not only is belief necessary for salvation, but Jesus specifically said that those who do not believe will be lost. He said elsewhere, *"Therefore I*

said to you that you will die in your sins; for unless you believe that I am He, you will die in your sins" (John 8:24). As we noted earlier, this means that we must not only believe in the existence of Jesus, but also that He is Deity (cf. Colossians 2:9).

- **Repent of sins** – "*I tell you, no, but unless you repent, you will all likewise perish*" (Luke 13:3, 5). The belief that we are to have must lead us to action. Repentance means to put away sin and begin serving the Lord. Jesus said elsewhere, "*If anyone wishes to come after Me, he must deny himself, and take up his cross daily and follow Me*" (Luke 9:23). When we make the decision to follow the Lord, we are making a commitment to serve Him *daily*.

- **Confess faith in Christ** – "*That if you confess with your mouth Jesus as Lord, and believe in your heart that God raised Him from the dead, you will be saved; for with the heart a person believes, resulting in righteousness, and with the mouth he confesses, resulting in salvation*" (Romans 10:9-10). This is the verbal affirmation of our faith. We must do more than mentally acknowledge the Lordship of Christ. In addition to repentance, we must also be willing to make "*the good confession in the presence of many witnesses*" (1 Timothy 6:12).

- **Be baptized into Christ** – "*He who has believed and has been baptized shall be saved; but he who has disbelieved shall be condemned*" (Mark 16:16). "*Go therefore and make disciples of all the nations, baptizing them in the name of the Father and the Son and the Holy Spirit*" (Matthew 28:19). Many people will push back on this point and try to argue that baptism is not necessary in order to be saved or to become a disciple of Jesus. Yet Jesus said that baptism is just as necessary for salvation as belief (Mark 16:16) and is an essential step in the discipleship process (Matthew 28:19). Those who reject this and have "*disbelieved*" Jesus "*shall be condemned*" (Mark 16:16). Paul described baptism as the act in which we put on Christ: "*For all of you who were baptized into Christ have clothed yourselves with Christ*" (Galatians 3:27).

When we become a disciple, we then *belong to Christ*. Peter explained this in his first epistle: "*But you are a chosen race, a royal priesthood, a holy nation, a people for God's own possession…for you once were not a people, but now you are the people of God…*" (1 Peter 2:9-10). As "*a people for His own possession,*" we must be "*zealous for good deeds*" (Titus 2:14). In other words, we must continue to serve Him and do what is right throughout our lives.

Conclusion

As we have seen in this lesson, the opportunity to become a disciple of Jesus is open to *everyone* (Matthew 28:19). It involves believing in Him and submitting to His will in all things (John 8:24, 31; Matthew 28:20). The reward for serving Him as a disciple is freedom from sin (John 8:32-36) and, ultimately, eternal salvation (Hebrews 5:9).

Are you truly a disciple of Christ? If not, you can be one. Whether you need to *begin* your life as one of His disciples or you need to *return* to faithful service, you can do it; and we would love to help you take the steps you need to take in order to faithfully follow the Lord.

More About Jesus

Christ Our Mediator

One of the ways that Jesus is described in the New Testament is as a *mediator*. Paul wrote, "*For there is one God, and one mediator also between God and men, the man Christ Jesus*" (1 Timothy 2:5). It is important that we understand what this means. Let us consider what the New Testament teaches about Jesus as our mediator.

What Is a Mediator?

The word translated *mediator* means "a go-between" (Vine's). It is used two ways in the New Testament:

1. **One who mediates between two parties to produce peace** – Paul identified the two parties as "*God and men*" (1 Timothy 2:5).
2. **One who acts as a guarantee to secure something that would otherwise not be obtained** – In this case, what Jesus secured were the terms of the new covenant. "*For this reason He is the mediator of a new covenant, so that, since a death has taken place for the redemption of the transgressions that were committed under the first covenant, those who have been called may receive*

the promise of the eternal inheritance" (Hebrews 9:15).

So as it is described in the New Testament, what does the role of *mediator* entail? A mediator is one who brings two parties together to secure a covenant between them. This is what Christ has done for us.

Jesus' Qualifications to Be Our Mediator

Paul said there is *"one mediator...the man Christ Jesus"* (1 Timothy 2:5). Jesus was the *only one* who could fulfill this role. He was qualified because he shared characteristics of both parties.

The deity of Jesus – John began his gospel with this statement about Jesus: *"In the beginning was the Word, and the Word was with God, and the Word was God"* (John 1:1). While on earth, Jesus indicated that He was equal with the Father. When He said, *"My Father is working until now, and I Myself am working,"* the Jews correctly understood Him to be *"making Himself equal with God"* by *"calling God His own Father"* (John 5:17-18). Jesus said elsewhere, *"I and the Father are one"* (John 10:30). Paul told the Colossians, *"For in Him all the fullness of Deity dwells in bodily form"* (Colossians 2:9), clearly indicating that Jesus was God in the flesh.

The humanity of Jesus – Paul emphasized this point by referring to Him as *"the **man** Christ Jesus"* (1 Timothy 2:5). While *"the Word was with God, and...was God"* (John 1:1), Jesus also *"became flesh, and dwelt among us"* (John 1:14). He took on *"the form of a bond-servant"* and was *"made in the *likeness of men*" and was "*found in appearance as a man*" (Philippians 2:7-8). Because He lived as one of us, we can have confidence in Him as our "*high priest*" because we know with certainty that He can "*sympathize with our weaknesses*" since He "*has been tempted in all things as we are, yet without sin*" (Hebrews 4:15).

Jesus was qualified to serve as the mediator between God and men because He shared characteristics of both God and men.

What Jesus Did in His Work as Mediator

To understand what Jesus did in His work as mediator, we need to remember the two ways in which the term *mediator* is used in the New Testament:

1. One who mediates between two parties to produce peace.
2. One who acts as a guarantee to secure something that would otherwise not be obtained.

Jesus brought about peace between man and God through His death on the cross. In fulfilling the role as the "*mediator,*" Jesus "*gave Himself as a ransom for all*" (1 Timothy 2:5-6). The word *ransom* describes "what is given in exchange for another as the price of his redemption" (Thayer). This was what Jesus did when He died on the cross. Peter wrote, "*Knowing that you were not redeemed with perishable things like silver or gold from your futile way of life inherited from your forefathers, but with precious blood, as of a lamb unblemished and spotless, the blood of Christ*" (1 Peter

1:18-19). Paul explained that it was through Christ that the Father would *"reconcile all things to Himself, having made peace through the blood of His cross...He has now reconciled you in His fleshly body through death..."* (Colossians 1:20-22). The sacrifice of Jesus on the cross, in which He offered His body and shed His blood, made reconciliation possible between God and men. This sacrifice was part of His work as our mediator because it allowed the two parties to be brought back together.

In His death, Jesus did more than just bring peace – **He also ratified the conditions of peace** (the covenant). The Hebrew writer said, *"For this reason He is the mediator of a new covenant, so that, since a death has taken place for the redemption of the transgressions that were committed under the first covenant, those who have been called may receive the promise of the eternal inheritance"* (Hebrews 9:15). The death of Jesus was a *"necessity"* for this because *"a covenant is valid only when men are dead, for it is never in force while the one who made it lives"* (Hebrews 9:16-17). This new covenant was *"enacted on better promises"* (Hebrews 8:6) as we look forward to the reward of heaven.

The Benefits of Having Jesus as Our Mediator

As the work of a mediator involved two primary functions, there are two primary benefits for those who will submit themselves to the Lord's covenant.

First, we have peace with God. Paul said that in Christ *"we have redemption through His blood, the forgiveness of our trespasses"* (Ephesians 1:7). Our sin separates us from God

(Isaiah 59:2), but the blood of Christ allows us to be reconciled to Him (Romans 5:9-10). Since we have peace with God, we also have access *"to the throne of grace"* (Hebrews 4:16) and the hope of salvation (1 Timothy 2:4-6).

Second, we have a covenant that has been guaranteed. We know what to do to be right with God through the gospel that has been revealed. Paul explained, *"For in it the righteousness of God is revealed from faith to faith; as it is written, 'But the righteous man shall live by faith'"* (Romans 1:17). The gospel shows us how to live by faith. Furthermore, we know that the terms of the gospel will not be changed. It has been given *"once for all time"* (Jude 3, NLT). Because this covenant is guaranteed, we have the hope of salvation. As the Hebrew writer explained, *"It is impossible for God to lie"*; therefore, we have *"a hope both sure and steadfast and one which enters within the veil, where Jesus has entered as a forerunner for us"* (Hebrews 6:18-20). The new covenant with its *"better promises"* (Hebrews 8:6) has been given. We can trust in God's promises.

Conclusion

The bottom line is this – we have the hope of salvation because of Jesus' work as our *mediator*. He brought about peace between man and God. He also guaranteed the covenant with its better promises. Knowing this, we need to be sure we submit to the terms of the covenant so that we can take advantage of the promises contained in it.

The Shepherd and the Sheep

Jesus described Himself as *"the good shepherd [who] lays down His life for the sheep"* (John 10:11). A shepherd provides guidance, sustenance, and protection for the flock. No one is able to provide the same care for us as Jesus. He *willingly* sacrificed Himself for us (John 10:17-18). Therefore, it is vitally important that we have Christ as our shepherd.

How do we become one of His sheep? And how do we remain in His fold? Notice what Jesus said:

> *"My sheep hear My voice, and I know them, and they follow Me"* (John 10:27).

Let us briefly examine this phrase to see how we can take advantage of the care provided by the Good Shepherd.

"My Sheep Hear My Voice"

If we want to have Jesus as our shepherd, we must be willing to listen. On another occasion, Jesus said, *"He who has ears to hear, let him hear"* (Luke 8:8). Many have ears to hear, but refuse to listen (cf. Acts 7:57). A willingness to listen requires humility (James 1:21), as we must recognize that we do not have all of the answers and need the Lord's instruction (cf. Jeremiah 10:23). We must also have a desire to learn, just as the Bereans who *"received the word with great eagerness"* (Acts 17:11).

Hearing the Lord's voice also requires a respect for Him and His authority. Jesus said, *"All authority has been given to Me"* (Matthew 28:18). A proper respect for His authority (godly fear) will motivate us to hear and understand His teaching. The wise man said, *"The fear of the Lord is the beginning of knowledge"* (Proverbs 1:7). If one does not fear the Lord, he will see no reason to hear His words; therefore, he will not grow in knowledge of those things that have been revealed from above.

Not only do the sheep *hear* His voice, they also *"know His voice"* (John 10:4). In other words, if we are to be of the Lord's flock, we must be able to recognize His teaching and distinguish it from the teachings of men. The gospel message is distinct (cf. Acts 17:20; 1 Corinthians 14:7-8). We must be able to distinguish it from the errors of denominationalism and liberalism. John wrote, *"Beloved, do not believe every spirit, but test the spirits to see whether they are from God, because many false prophets have gone out into the world"* (1 John 4:1). We must be careful to follow the words of Christ and His apostles rather than being led astray by others.

"I Know Them"

Paul told Timothy, *"The Lord knows those who are His,"* and that this is a *"firm foundation"* for us (2 Timothy 2:19). He told the brethren in Corinth, *"If anyone loves God, he is known by Him"* (1 Corinthians 8:3). How do we show our love for God? We do so by keeping His commandments (1 John 5:3). Therefore, if we want the Lord to *know* us, we must *obey* Him.

More than simply *knowing* His sheep, the Lord has *foreknown* them. Paul wrote about this predestination in his letter to Ephesus: *"Just as He chose us in Him before the foundation of the world, that we would be holy and blameless before Him. In love He predestined us to adoption as sons through Jesus Christ to Himself, according to the kind intention of His will"* (Ephesians 1:4-5). Paul was not teaching the Calvinistic concept of predestination – that God has chosen certain individuals for salvation. Rather, God has predestined a *class* of people – those who would be holy and blameless.

We can be assured that God notices us when we *"keep His commandments"* and live in a *"holy and blameless"* manner (1 John 5:3; Ephesians 1:4). Jesus is the Good Shepherd; He will not forget us (cf. Hebrews 6:9-10). He is distinguished from the *"hired hand"* in that He has a personal interest in us and was willing to lay down His life for us (John 10:13-15). However, if He does not know us, we will be lost (Matthew 7:23). Our salvation depends upon the Lord *knowing* us.

"They Follow Me"

The conditions we must meet for salvation include more than just a knowledge of God's word and belief in Christ. To have Christ as our shepherd, we must *follow* Him (cf. Psalm 23:2). The shepherd leads, but the sheep must follow.

Following the Lord requires faithful obedience. We cannot be saved by *"faith alone"* (James 2:24). James wrote, *"For just as the body without the spirit is dead, so also faith without works is dead"* (James 2:26). We must follow Christ to be of his flock. Jesus asked, *"Why do you call Me, 'Lord, Lord,' and do not do what I say?"* (Luke 6:46). He is not our Lord if we do not obey Him.

Wandering away from the Lord leads to disaster, as we can no longer enjoy the protection of the shepherd against our *"adversary, the devil, [who] prowls around like a roaring lion, seeking someone to devour"* (1 Peter 5:8). We are safe as long as we remain in the fold. After saying that His sheep follow Him, Jesus said, *"No one will snatch them out of My hand. My Father, who has given them to Me, is greater than all; and no one is able to snatch them out of the Father's hand"* (John 10:28-29). As long as we follow the Lord, we are safe; but when we turn away from following Him, we are not.

Conclusion

This verse – *"My sheep hear My voice, and I know them, and they follow Me"* (John 10:27) – concisely contains the plan of salvation:

- We must hear the word of the Lord (Luke 8:8; Romans 10:17).
- We must be known by Him – obey His commandments to become part of His flock (John 8:24; Luke 13:3, 5; Mark 16:16).
- We must follow Him – continue in faithful service (Revelation 2:10; Hebrews 5:9).

We do not need to worry about Jesus doing what is necessary to save us (John 10:11, 28). He has taken care of His part. We must do our part to become part of His flock and remain in it.

Jesus Christ: Prince of Peace

> *"For a child will be born to us, a son will be given to us; and the government will rest on His shoulders; and His name will be called Wonderful Counselor, Mighty God, Eternal Father, Prince of Peace"* (Isaiah 9:6).

There are many terms and titles used to describe Jesus throughout the Bible. A few are found in the passage above. Isaiah, in prophesying of the birth of the Messiah, spoke of Jesus' wisdom, power, deity, and eternity. But notice the last name – *"Prince of Peace."* Jesus is the one who would bring peace. After His birth, the heavenly host proclaimed, *"Glory to God in the highest, and on earth peace among men with whom He is pleased"* (Luke 2:14).

Jesus came to the earth to bring peace. But what kind of peace did He come to bring? It was one that only He could bring, one that man could not obtain on his own, and one that had been missing. Jesus came to bring peace between man and God (Romans 5:1). This had been missing because of sin. Sin separates man from God (Isaiah 59:1-2). *"All have sinned*" (Romans 3:23) and man could do nothing on his own to remedy that (Ephesians 2:8-9). Notice what Paul wrote:

> *"For He Himself is our peace, who made both groups into one and broke down the barrier of the dividing wall, by abolishing in His flesh the enmity, which is the Law of commandments contained in ordinances, so that in Himself He might make the two into one new man, thus establishing peace, and might reconcile them both in one body to God through the cross, by it having put to death the enmity. And He came and preached peace to you who were far away, and peace to those who were near"* (Ephesians 2:14-17).

This passage teaches us a few things. First, this peace is available to all. It is open to *"both groups"* – Jews and Gentiles (Ephesians 2:14). Those who are *"far away"* (Gentiles) and those who are *"near"* (Jews) would be able to access this peace (Ephesians 2:17). Second, they would have peace as *"one new man."* They could not enjoy peace with God while remaining in their old sinful state. There must be a definite contrast between the *"old self"* and the *"new self"* (Colossians 3:9-10). There would have to be a change of life. Third, we see that the peace comes from being reconciled to God. They have peace in being brought back into a right relationship with Him. Finally, if they wanted to partake of this peace they had to be part of the *"one body."* This body is Christ's body, also referred to as the church (Ephesians 1:22-23). One becomes a part of this body by being *"baptized into Christ"* (Galatians 3:27; 1 Corinthians 12:13). So there are conditions that must be met to enjoy peace with God. But none of it would be possible without the work of Jesus Christ.

It is also important to note that Jesus did not come to establish peace among men. Consider what Jesus said:

> "*Do not think that I came to bring peace on the earth; I did not come to bring peace, but a sword. For I came to set a man against his father, and a daughter against her mother, and a daughter-in-law against her mother-in-law; and a man's enemies will be the members of his household*" (Matthew 10:34-36).

Jesus' purpose for coming to the earth was not to make peace among men. Peace among men may be a *byproduct* of the peace Jesus made available between man and God. But this passage teaches us that Jesus did not come for that purpose.

As Christians, we can have peace with those who have peace with God. Notice again what the angels proclaimed at the birth of Jesus: "*Glory to God in the highest, and on earth peace among men with whom He is pleased*" (Luke 2:14). Yes, there can be "*peace among men,*" but which men? Those "*with whom He is pleased.*" Those who "*walk in the Light as He Himself is in the Light*" (1 John 1:7). Also notice what Paul wrote: "*In Himself He might make the two into one new man, thus establishing peace, and might reconcile them both in one body to God through the cross.*" Jews and Gentiles were able to have peace with each other because both had been reconciled to God and were part of the "*one body*" – Christ's body, the church.

In following Christ, we are to "*pursue the things which make for peace*" (Romans 14:19). How do we do that? Do we overlook differences in matters of faith? Do we ignore sin and error? No! James said, "*The wisdom from above is first pure, then peaceable*" (James 3:17). The wisdom from above is that which was revealed by the Holy Spirit (1 Corinthians 2:7-13). It is the word of God. We cannot compromise or adulterate the teachings of Scripture so we can have peace with men. We are to "*preserve the unity of the Spirit in the bond of peace*" (Ephesians 4:3). If we have unity and peace at the expense of the truth revealed by the Spirit, we find ourselves guilty of condoning those in sin (2 John 9-11).

The context of Romans 14 was addressing our relationship with a "*brother*" (Romans 14:15). It discussed matters in which, no matter what his personal opinion may be, "*God has accepted him*" (Romans 14:3). Since God had accepted him, then we know that the difference that we have with him cannot be a matter of sin. Because it is not a matter of sin, but simply opinion, he enjoys peace with God. We are to make sure we have peace with those who also have peace with God. Paul wrote earlier in this letter, "*Be devoted to one another in brotherly love; give preference to one another in honor*" (Romans 12:10). He told the brethren in Philippi, "*Do nothing from selfishness or empty conceit, but with humility of mind regard one another as more important than yourselves; do not merely look out for your own personal interests, but also for the interest of others*" (Philippians 2:3-4). In the next few verses he went on to describe Christ's attitude – our Prince of Peace.

He humbled Himself for the benefit of others (Philippians 2:5-8). We should have humility when dealing with brothers and sisters in Christ so we can enjoy peace with one another.

What about those who are not Christians? Can we *"pursue the things which make for peace"* (Romans 14:19) with them too? We can. Paul wrote, *"If possible, so far as it depends on you, be at peace with all men"* (Romans 12:18). However, sometimes peace is not possible. But what is the best way to enjoy peace with them? First get them to have peace with God. That is why Jesus came to this earth. He came to bring about peace between man and God. We need to teach people and help them see what they need to do to partake of this peace and what they must do to continue in this peace. Then, when they too enjoy peace with God, we will all enjoy the byproduct of that – peace among men. Let us seek after the peace that Jesus came to bring, and in so doing, enjoy peace with those of like mind.

Jesus Christ: Our Perfect Example

> *"For you have been called for this purpose, since Christ also suffered for you, leaving you an example for you to follow in His steps, who committed no sin, nor was any deceit found in His mouth; and while being reviled, He did not revile in return; while suffering, He uttered no threats, but kept entrusting Himself to Him who judges righteously; and He Himself bore our sins in His body on the cross, so that we might die to sin and live to righteousness; for by His wounds you were healed"* (1 Peter 2:21-24).

In this passage, Peter explained that Jesus left an example for us to follow. There are many people we may look up to as examples in life – parents, peers, older Christians, successful individuals, and more. Yet Jesus was not just *an* example; He was the *perfect* example. This passage shows us how He left a perfect example for us.

An Example of *Suffering*

Peter began by saying, "*Christ also suffered for you, leaving you an example*" (1 Peter 2:21). Jesus knew He would die on the cross, even telling His disciples ahead of time that it would happen (Matthew 16:21); yet He did not try to avoid it. He knew *why* it was going to happen – He would suffer and die for *our* sins (1 Peter 2:24; Isaiah 53:4-5) – but He loved us enough to endure it. He even had the power to prevent His death, having authority to call down "*more than twelve legions of angels*" (Matthew 26:53-54); but He did not change His mind. He suffered beyond what any of us will ever have to endure. In doing so, he left an example for us.

The Christian life is one that will involve suffering. Paul told Timothy, "*Indeed, all who desire to live godly in Christ Jesus will be persecuted*" (2 Timothy 3:12). When we do what is right and suffer for it, we must patiently endure. Peter made this point right before emphasizing the perfect example of Jesus: "*For what credit is there if, when you sin and are harshly treated, you endure it with patience? But if when you do what is right and suffer for it you patiently endure it, this finds favor with God*" (1 Peter 2:20). As we face these hardships and trials, we must do so without abandoning our faith.

An Example of *Sinlessness*

While Jesus endured a horrible death on the cross along with all of the suffering that led up to it, He "*committed no sin, nor was any deceit found in His mouth*" (1 Peter 2:22). Even though all men have sinned (Romand 3:23), Jesus did not. When He was tempted, He used the Scriptures each time to resist (Matthew 4:1-11). The chief priests tried to *"obtain false testimony against Jesus,"* but they *"did not find any"* (Matthew 26:59-60). There was no reason to condemn Him to death or even to some lesser punishment.

We are to strive to follow Jesus' sinless example. John explained that this was the reason he wrote his first epistle: *"My little children, I am writing these things to you so that you may not sin..."* (1 John 2:1). When Jesus spoke with the woman who was allegedly caught in adultery, He told her, *"Go...sin no more"* (John 8:11). God has extended His grace to us, yet we must not use this as an excuse to sin. Evidently, some in Rome had this misconception. Paul sought to correct this when he wrote, *"What shall we say then? Are we to continue in sin so that grace may increase? May it never be! How shall we who died to sin still live in it?"* (Romans 6:1-2). If we are following Christ, we are to strive to overcome sin in our lives.

An Example of *Reliance upon God*

While Jesus endured suffering, He *"kept entrusting Himself to Him who judges righteously"* (1 Peter 2:23). When His enemies *"reviled"* Him, He did not respond in kind. Isaiah, prophesying of Jesus' suffering, said, *"He was oppressed and He was afflicted, yet He did not open His mouth; like a lamb that is led to slaughter, and like a sheep that is silent before its shearers, so He did not open His mouth"* (Isaiah 53:7). He came to do the Father's will (John 6:38) and relied upon the Father for help in carrying out His work (Luke 22:42-43).

We have been called to do the will of God. Jesus said that the one who *"does the will of My Father"* will *"enter the king-*

dom of heaven" (Matthew 7:21). As we strive to do His will, we must "*trust in the Lord with all* [our] *heart and do not lean on* [our] *own understanding*" (Proverbs 3:5). As we face suffering in this life, let us trust in God and the hope that He offers. Paul described his attitude when he "*despaired even of life; indeed, we had the sentence of death within ourselves so that we would not trust in ourselves, but in God who raises the dead*" (2 Corinthians 1:8-9). As we face difficulties and circumstances beyond our control, we need to recognize our dependence upon God and rely on Him.

An Example of *Sacrifice*

Jesus "*bore our sins in His body on the cross*" (1 Peter 2:24). As we already noticed, Jesus did not go to the cross on account of His own sins (1 Peter 2:22); He died for our sins. Peter explained later in this same epistle, "*For Christ also died for sins once for all, the just for the unjust*" (1 Peter 3:18). He freely gave His life as a sacrifice for us (John 10:17-18). As Paul explained in his letter to the saints in Rome, Jesus died for us while we were "*helpless*," "*sinners*," and "*enemies*" of God (Romans 5:6, 8, 10).

Because of His willingness to sacrifice for us, we must be willing to sacrifice our lives for Him. Paul told the Romans, "*Therefore I urge you, brethren, by the mercies of God, to present your bodies a living and holy sacrifice, acceptable to God, which is your spiritual service of worship*" (Romans 12:1). We should be able to echo the words of the apostle: "*I have been crucified with Christ; and it is no longer I who live, but Christ lives in me; and the life which I now live in the flesh I live by faith in the Son of God, who loved me and gave Him-*

self up for me" (Galatians 2:20). John pointed out that this also means we should be willing to sacrifice for our brethren: *"We know love by this, that He laid down His life for us; and we ought to lay down our lives for the brethren"* (1 John 3:16). We need to put the Lord and others ahead of our own personal interests and be willing to make sacrifices.

Conclusion

As Peter concluded this section, he reminded us of how we had strayed from the Lord: *"For you were continually straying like sheep, but now you have returned to the Shepherd and Guardian of your souls"* (1 Peter 2:25). Now that we are following Him, we must stay with Him. If we stray again, we must return to Him as our Shepherd and Guardian – our leader and protector. Let us submit our lives to Him and follow His *perfect* example.

Jesus: The Great Debater

One aspect about Jesus that is often ignored is His ability to debate. There is a reason for this. To say that religious debates are not popular in our time is an understatement. Yet the ability to debate is a valuable skill for those who would endeavor to teach the gospel to others. Jesus was so effective that Luke recorded four occasions in just one chapter (Luke 20) in which Jesus silenced His opponents. He did so by presenting arguments that could not be combated.

Paul described the work of spreading the gospel as "*destroying speculation and every lofty thing raised up against the knowledge of God, and we are taking every thought captive to the obedience of Christ*" (2 Corinthians 10:5). We are not to try to force anyone or trick anyone into obeying the gospel. We *persuade* people by dismantling the arguments used against the truth.

When Jesus silenced His opponents four times in Luke 20, He was able to do so without turning the common people against Him (Luke 19:48; 21:38). We must develop our abilities to confound our opponents while also persuading the people. In order to help us do this, let us notice *how* Jesus silenced His opponents.

He Appealed to Divine Authority

The chief priests, scribes and elders asked Jesus a question: *"Tell us by what authority You are doing these things, or who is the one who gave You this authority?"* (Luke 20:2). This came right after Jesus' triumphal entry into Jerusalem in which He received praise from the people (Luke 19:37-38) and after His cleansing of the temple (Luke 19:45-46). It is likely that their question, at least in part, had to do with these things.

Their question is actually a legitimate one. It is important to question the basis for why things are done. Jesus, in His response, identified two sources of authority – *"from heaven or from men"* (Luke 20:4). There was no other option. We must have divine authority for all that we say and do (Colossians 3:17). So their question and Jesus' follow-up are good for us to ask today.

However, we learn in the account that the ones who questioned Jesus were not really interested in divine authority. They simply questioned Jesus about authority in hopes that they might find an accusation against Him. We know they were not interested in discussing divine authority because of their refusal to answer Jesus' question (Luke 20:5-7). They were more concerned with the consequences of their answer than with the truth. So all they could say is that *"they did not know"* (Luke 20:7).

We may receive similar questions today. By what authority do you teach against homosexuality? By what authority to you discipline a brother living in sin? Like Jesus, we must determine whether those asking the questions are sincere or are just wanting to stir up problems. Do they really care about divine authority? We can ask questions like Jesus did to find out. We should be more than willing to defend our teachings and practices by the word of God. We expect others to do the same. So we make appeals to divine authority. Those who are interested in truth will learn. Those who are not – like the chief priests, scribes, and elders – will eventually become silent.

He Provided Clear Explanations

Jesus was later asked about the lawfulness of paying taxes (Luke 20:20-26). "*Is it lawful for us to pay taxes to Caesar, or not?*" (Luke 20:22). They were trying to trap Jesus, looking for some cause whereby they could "deliver Him to the rule and the authority of the governor" (Luke 20:20).

If Jesus had given a simple "yes" or "no" answer, they may have been able to use that against Him. If Jesus had simply said, "Yes, it is lawful to pay taxes to Caesar," they could have tried to turn the people against Him, given the general disdain for the Roman rulers – which even included those who would collect taxes for them. If Jesus said, "No, it is not lawful to pay taxes to Caesar" (which seems to be what they hoped He would say), they could have gone to the authorities and accused Jesus of leading a movement against the rulers, inciting the people to rebellion and telling them to not pay their taxes.

Jesus did not fall for their trap. Instead, He gave a clear explanation to their question (Luke 20:24-25). The money bore the image of Caesar. Therefore, it was lawful to pay taxes. But He went on to make the point that we must likewise give back to God that which belongs to Him. Similarly, this is that which bears His likeness – our own selves (cf. Genesis 1:26-27). As a result of this clear response, *"they became silent"* (Luke 20:26).

People may try to trap us today by looking for a simple "yes" or "no" answer to their question. In such cases, we must give a clear explanation. Suppose someone asks the question: "Will only members of the church of Christ be saved?" Simply answering "yes" or "no" can give them cause to speak against us. So it would be wise to give a clear, yet concise, explanation. There is salvation in no one but Jesus (Acts 4:12). He is the Savior of the church (Ephesians 5:23) and purchased it with His blood (Acts 20:28). Therefore, if we want to be saved, we need to be part of that one church (Matthew 16:18).

He Avoided Speculation

Next, Jesus was confronted by the Sadducees with a question about the resurrection (Luke 20:28-33). They presented a scenario in which one woman was married to seven men. Their question was this: *"In the resurrection therefore, which one's wife will she be? For all seven had married her"* (Luke 20:33).

The Sadducees were not asking this question out of sincerity. They did not even believe in the resurrection (Luke

20:27). They were not seeking answers. Rather, they tried to delve into the realm of speculation to make it look like the truth about the resurrection was not so certain. When Jesus answered their question, He did not remind them about what was written in the Law (Luke 20:34-36). This was not something they could have known, or even was pertinent to keeping the Old Law. So God said nothing about the fact that in *"the resurrection,"* people *"neither marry nor are given in marriage"* (Luke 20:35). Only Jesus, who had been in heaven and was God in the flesh, could have answered this question this way. Based on the Old Testament Scriptures, men could only speculate about this question.

Jesus only briefly addressed their question. He then went on to discuss the primary issue – their belief that there was no resurrection (Luke 20:37-38). In doing this, He quoted a passage from the Law (Exodus 3:6) and made His point from that. He did not waste time over speculation. He went directly to the sure and certain truth that they needed to accept.

People who do not like the truth will try to steer the discussion toward speculation. Paul said we must avoid this (1 Timothy 1:4). But this is often done when discussing the necessity of baptism. Someone will ask, "What if someone is on their way to the church building to be baptized and they get in a car accident and die on the way. Will God send that person to hell?" Ultimately, God is the judge (2 Corinthians 5:10). All we know is what the Bible says: *"He who has believed and has been baptized shall be saved"* (Mark 16:16). *"Baptism now saves you"* (1 Peter 3:21).

We cannot speculate about what God has not revealed (cf. Deuteronomy 29:29). Yet people speculate today and then use their speculation as an excuse to disobey. We must avoid speculation and focus on the truth.

He Directed People Toward a Conclusion

Finally, instead of being asked a question, Jesus asked, *"How is it that they say the Christ is David's son? For David himself says in the book of Psalms, 'The Lord said to my Lord, "Sit at My right hand, until I make your enemies a footstool for Your feet."' Therefore David calls Him 'Lord,' and how is He his son?"* (Luke 20:41-44).

The Christ was certainly to descend from David (2 Samuel 7:12-13). The Jews understood this. In Matthew's account, Jesus first asked, *"What do you think about the Christ, whose son is He?"* They responded, *"The son of David"* (Matthew 22:42). So *"if David calls Him Lord, how is He his son?"* (Matthew 22:45).

Jesus asked a question for which there was only one answer. They knew the Christ would descend from David. Yet, David called Him Lord. How can these facts be reconciled? Jesus later said, *"I am the root and the descendant of David"* (Revelation 22:16). Jesus was not just a man. He was God in the flesh. This conclusion was unavoidable if they were willing to accept it. Of course, the Pharisees were not; so the text says, *"No one was able to answer Him a word, nor did anyone dare from that day on to ask Him another question"* (Matthew 22:46).

We must learn how to lead people to the truth in such a way so that the right conclusion is unavoidable. We should not encourage people to be comfortable in their current situation if they need to change. We should not lead them down an unclear path that could easily result in them accepting some denominational error or becoming more firmly entrenched in it. There is *one truth* (cf. John 14:6). We must direct people to that truth. It is alright to make people think. The only way people will be truly converted is if their faith is their own.

Conclusion

It is good to learn lessons like these from Jesus, the Master Teacher, so we can be better prepared to teach others. All Christians have opportunities from time to time to share the gospel. Most people will not be quick to accept the truth. Some will even oppose it. In either case, we must learn to effectively demonstrate the irrefutable truth of the gospel so that those who are honest will have opportunity to come to understand the will of God.

The Way, the Truth, and the Life

Jesus said, "I am the way, and the truth, and the life; no one comes to the Father but through Me" (John 14:6). This simple, concise statement reveals some important truths.

Jesus is the Way – He is the path we are to take. He left *"an example for* [us] *to follow in His steps"* (1 Peter 2:21). This is not necessarily an easy path. After all, the example He left was one of *"no sin"* (1 Peter 2:22). To be Christ-like, we must strive for perfection (Matthew 5:48). John wrote *"so that you may not sin"* (1 John 2:1). Of course, there are provisions made if we do sin (1 John 2:1; Acts 8:22); but the goal is perfection.

Just as Jesus did, we must take up our cross (Luke 9:23). This means we must sacrifice our life (Romans 12:1) and live for Him. *"A man's way is not in himself"* (Jeremiah 10:23). We must follow the way of Christ.

Jesus is the Truth – Later, Jesus said that the word of God is truth (John 17:17). Jesus was the Word in the flesh (John 1:1, 14). He came *"to testify to the truth"* (John 18:37).

The word and message that Jesus taught was true because it came from the source of truth – Jesus Christ Himself.

Notice that Jesus said He was "*the truth*" – one truth, not one of many. Truth is not subjective. God and His word are right no matter what we say or think about it (Romans 3:4). We must simply believe and accept what God has said. His word (the truth) will be the standard by which we will be judged (John 12:48).

Jesus is the Life – Jesus came that we "*may have life, and have it abundantly*" (John 10:10). This abundant life is not the "health and wealth gospel" that many false teachers proclaim. It is "*that which is life indeed*" (1 Timothy 6:19) – eternal life. Jesus' mission in coming to earth was to reconcile man to God (Ephesians 2:16; Romans 5:10-11). To do this, He had to deal with the problem that caused the separation – sin (Isaiah 59:1-2). In dealing with the problem of sin, He made eternal life possible (Romans 6:23).

There is No Other Way – After stating that He was the way, truth, and life, Jesus said, "*No one comes to the Father but through Me*" (John 14:6). If we want to get to the Father, it must be through Christ (Ephesians 2:18). Peter said, "*There is salvation in no one else; for there is no other name under heaven that has been given among men by which we must be saved*" (Acts 4:12).

Are you willing to follow His way, accept His truth, so you can have life in Him?

Another Jesus

There are certain times of the year when the religious world pays special attention to Jesus. One is the Christmas season in which they celebrate the birth of Christ. The other is Easter when they focus on His death and resurrection.

Why is there such a focus on these things about Jesus? Remembering a baby Jesus reminds people of the grace of God in sending Him to earth – not to mention the fact that nearly everyone loves babies. In the death and resurrection of Christ, we see a Savior who died for our sins and gives us the hope of heaven. It is no wonder why people celebrate these events. These things make people feel good. Anymore in religion, if something makes people feel good, that is what they choose to believe and practice.

But the Bible has much more to say about Jesus than just these things. Sure, we must remember the birth, death, and resurrection of Jesus. But by only focusing on these things and ignoring so much of what the Bible teaches about the Christ, many in the religious world have accepted *another* Jesus (2 Corinthians 11:4). They have molded Him to suit their desires. For this study, let us consider some of the other things the word of God has to say about Jesus that many have forgotten, ignored, or have never known.

The Jesus Many Do Not Know

He is the one who drove the moneychangers out of the temple – John recorded that near the time of the Passover, Jesus went into the temple and found moneychangers and some who were selling sheep, oxen, and doves. He then made a scourge of cords (a whip), drove out the ones selling the animals, and overturned the moneychangers' tables. He was upset because they had made His Father's house *"a place of business."* The disciples remembered a prophecy that explained why He acted in this way: *"Zeal for your house will consume me"* (John 2:13-17).

This does not fit with many people's concept of a meek, gentle, and loving Savior. But does Jesus' love negate His zeal for the Lord's house? No, it does not. We see the point in this that our worship to God matters. Even though Jesus *"loved [us] and gave Himself up for us"* (Ephesians 5:2), He still taught that we *"must worship in spirit and truth"* (John 4:24). These things that Jesus condemned were connected with the worship of God. They were not acts of worship themselves, but these men had mixed what was a legitimate business activity (cf. Deuteronomy 14:24-26) with worship and the place where people assembled to worship. By doing this they stood condemned. Some of our brethren today have not been careful in this regard and have mixed their business of selling books with Christians gathering together for worship. We see Jesus' attitude toward such actions in this passage. We must not corrupt or pervert our worship to God, even with activities that are wholesome and good at other times. The Jesus that many do not know demands that we do not adulterate the worship of God with other activities.

He is the one who drove people away – How many times have brethren complained that we are driving people away? Yet this is what Jesus did at times. In John 6, Jesus began with thousands of followers (John 6:10). But after teaching them some things they thought were *"difficult"* (John 6:60), *"many of His disciples withdrew and were not walking with Him anymore"* (John 6:66). After starting with thousands, He was left with only twelve (John 6:67), and one of these would eventually betray Him. Through His teaching, Jesus drove these people away.

So many in religion put such a high importance on numbers. They believe that numeric growth is an indicator of spiritual growth. But this is not always the case. If a church grows numerically, it is not always because it is growing spiritually. Our politically correct society goes to great lengths to *not* offend. So the churches that are growing are often the ones who try not to offend anyone. But the truth is sometimes offensive to people. Jesus offended people with His teaching (Matthew 15:12-14). Sometimes we must teach things that people will not like so that they might hear the truth, repent of their sin, and turn to God (2 Corinthians 7:8-10). Jesus valued the souls of others enough to teach the truth, regardless of how they might react to it. We must have the same attitude today.

He is the one who causes division – Jesus said, *"Do not think that I came to bring peace on the earth; I did not come to bring peace, but a sword. For I came to set a man against his father, and a daughter against her mother, and a daughter-in-law against her mother-in-law; and a man's enemies will be the members of his household"* (Matthew 10:34-36). Many desire unity at all costs. Denominational distinctions are being blurred. People just want to be able to get along. The Christmas holy day is used to promote peace and unity among men, just as the angels announced at Jesus' birth, *"On earth peace, goodwill toward men"* (Luke 2:14). But the peace Jesus came to bring was between man and God – reconciliation that was necessary because of our sins against God (Ephesians 2:13-18; Isaiah 59:2). Peace among men may be a byproduct of the peace between man and God, but it was not Jesus' primary purpose. He *"did not come to bring peace, but a sword"* (Matthew 10:34).

We should all desire unity (Psalm 133:1), but there are times when it is not possible. Paul told the Corinthians, *"For there must also be factions among you, so that those who are approved may become evident among you"* (1 Corinthians 11:19). How do we know when the time has come when there must be divisions or factions among us? When Jesus is the reason for the division (Matthew 10:34). When Jesus and His word teach one thing, and man teaches something else, there must be division. We are to be united on the basis of God's word (John 17:20-21). We cannot have fellowship with those who do not submit to the word of God (2 John 9-11). If we want to follow the Lord, we cannot sacrifice the truth in order to achieve or maintain unity.

He is the one who demands obedience – The idea many have of Jesus is that He will reward even those who fail to obey His instructions. While Jesus is willing to save all men (Romans 10:13), He will only save those who obey His will. In giving the Great Commission, Jesus told His apostles, *"Go therefore and make disciples of all the nations, baptizing them* *in the name of the Father and the Son and the Holy Spirit, teaching them to observe all that I commanded you"* (Matthew 28:19-20). Those who wish to be Christ's disciples are to be taught to do *all* that He commanded, not just *some* of what He commanded. We are not at liberty to pick and choose what commands and instructions we wish to obey.

At the end of Matthew 11, Jesus gave what is sometimes called the Lord's invitation. He said, *"Come to Me, all who are weary and heavy-laden, and I will give you rest"* (Matthew 11:28). It is a common idea that we invite Jesus to us (saying the "sinner's prayer"), but instead we must come to Him. If we wish to come to Him, He told us what we must do. *"Take My yoke upon you and learn from Me"* (Matthew 11:29). In taking on His yoke, we must allow Him to direct and guide us. We no longer do what we desire, but what He desires. Many people call Jesus "Lord," but do not treat Him as such. Calling Him Lord means we must follow His word. He asked the question, *"Why do you call Me, 'Lord, Lord,' and do not do what I say?"* (Luke 6:46). Jesus demands obedience from His followers. We must obey Him in order to be saved. He is *"to all those who obey Him the source of eternal salvation"* (Hebrews 5:9).

He is the one who will judge us – Paul wrote, *"For we must all appear before the judgment seat of Christ, so that each one may be recompensed for his deeds in the body, according to what he has done, whether good or bad"* (2 Corinthians 5:10). The Lord will judge each one of us according to what *we* have done, not what *He* has done. Some hold to the notion of imputed righteousness. This is the idea that the righteousness of Christ is imputed to us and, therefore, we are saved. But Jesus already did His part to make salvation possible. Now we must do our part. So He will judge us by the infallible standard of His word (John 12:48).

He is the one who will destroy the wicked – Paul wrote to the Thessalonians to comfort and encourage them in the face of persecution. He told them what Jesus would do when He returned. He said, *"The Lord Jesus will be revealed from heaven with His mighty angels in flaming fire, dealing out retribution to those who do not know God and to those who do not obey the gospel of our Lord Jesus. These will pay the penalty of eternal destruction, away from the presence of the Lord and from the glory of His power"* (2 Thessalonians 1:7-9). Many have asked the question, how can a loving God send anyone to hell? A similar question is how can a loving Lord destroy the wicked? The reason is because of His righteousness and justice (2 Thessalonians 1:5-6). Yes, Jesus loves us and wants us to be saved. That is why He has given us time to prepare to meet Him. But He will destroy those who do not obey Him. They will be told, *"Depart from Me, accursed ones, into the eternal fire which has been prepared for the devil and his angels"* (Matthew 25:41).

Conclusion

This Jesus that we have considered here is different from the one that many people claim to know. But it is this Jesus, and only this Jesus, who can provide salvation. *"And there is salvation in no one else; for there is no other name under heaven that has been given among men by which we must be saved"* (Acts 4:12). Let us not be deceived into following another

Jesus. Let us follow the one shown to us in the pages of God's word.

Testifying of Christ

After the Jews began persecuting Jesus for healing a man on the Sabbath (John 5:16), Jesus began discussing His equality with the Father (John 5:17-23), the future resurrection (John 5:25-29), and the proof that He was who He claimed to be (John 5:33-47). This final point was critical. Not every claim that one may make of himself is true. This was why Jesus said, "*If I alone testify about Myself, My testimony is not true*" (John 5:31). He was not saying that He might make false claims. After all, He "*always*" did the will of the Father (John 8:29). Yet there was a difference between what Jesus claimed about Himself and what others – His enemies, in particular – claimed about Him.

How could the people know that Jesus was the Christ and not an imposter? They would need to have *evidence*. Jesus explained that this evidence came in the form of *witness testimony* that verified His claims. In this passage, He described four witnesses that testified of Him and confirmed His claim as the Christ, the Son of God. Let us notice these briefly.

John the Baptist

"*You have sent to John, and he has testified to the truth. But the testimony which I receive is not from man, but I say these things so that you may be saved. He was the lamp that was burning and was shining and you were willing to rejoice for a while in his light"* (John 5:33-35).

When John saw Jesus approaching, he announced, *"Behold, the Lamb of God who takes away the sin of the world!"* (John 1:29). In this statement, he was providing clear, unmistakable testimony regarding Jesus' identity. The next day when he was with two of his disciples, he saw Jesus and repeated the same thing with the result that these men left John and started following Jesus (John 1:35-37). He wanted to make sure they knew the truth about Jesus instead of just hoping they might figure it out on their own.

This testimony was not coming from some obscure individual; instead, everyone was familiar with John. Matthew recorded, *"Then Jerusalem was going out to him, and all Judea and all the district around the Jordan; and they were being baptized by him in the Jordan River, as they confessed their sins"* (Matthew 3:5-6).

Not only were they familiar with John, they could also see in him someone of integrity. Jesus said that *"among those born of women there has not arisen anyone greater than John the Baptist"* (Matthew 11:11). He was not preaching for his own personal gain. He was *"in the wilderness"* and wore *"a garment of camel's hair and a leather belt around his waist; and his food was locusts and wild honey"* (Matthew 3:1, 4). As we already noted, he directed his own disciples to follow Jesus (John 1:35-37). He was not trying to amass a large following for himself; rather, he was pointing people to Jesus and making great sacrifices to do so. There was nothing for him to gain – from a worldly standpoint – by pointing people to Jesus and declaring Him to be the Lamb of God if it were not true.

Miracles

> *"But the testimony which I have is greater than the testimony of John; for the works which the Father has given Me to accomplish—the very works that I do—testify about Me, that the Father has sent Me"* (John 5:36).

The purpose of miracles was to produce faith. Near the end of his gospel, John wrote, *"Therefore many other signs Jesus also performed in the presence of the disciples, which are not written in this book; but these have been written so that you may believe that Jesus is the Christ, the Son of God; and that believing you may have life in His name"* (John 20:30-31). When the leaders challenged Jesus to tell them *"plainly"* if He was the Christ, He pointed to *"the works"* that He did (John 10:24-25) – which would include the miracles He performed – to prove that He was the Christ.

The gospel of John records several miracles that reveal certain things about Jesus:

- Jesus turned water to wine (John 2:1-11) – In having the servants fill the pots to the brim, He demonstrated that this was a genuine miracle and not some trick.

- Jesus healed a nobleman's son (John 4:46-54) – This miracle showed that He had the power to heal a specific person from a long distance.
- Jesus healed a lame man (John 5:1-9) – The account compared the work attributed to an angel to the better work of Christ.
- Jesus fed five thousand (John 6:1-14) – He created food for them, providing something that was superior to the manna that was provided for their forefathers in the wilderness.
- Jesus walked on water (John 6:15-21) – He was able to set aside the natural law of gravity.
- Jesus healed a blind man (John 9:1-7) – This individual was blind from birth, so it was not a temporary condition; yet this did not hinder Jesus from being able to grant him the gift of sight.
- Jesus raised Lazarus from the dead (John 11:1-44) – Rather than hurrying to him when He was informed that he was sick, Jesus waited until he was dead. When He finally arrived at Lazarus' tomb, the body would have already started decaying; yet Jesus was still able to raise him from the dead.

As John explained, these signs proved that *"Jesus is the Christ, the Son of God"* (John 20:31). If that were not true, He would not have been able to perform these miracles.

God the Father

"And the Father who sent Me, He has testified of Me. You have neither heard His voice at any time nor seen His form. You do not have

> *His word abiding in you, for you do not believe Him whom He sent*" (John 5:37-38).

When Jesus came to John to be baptized of him, the Father provided this testimony of Jesus from heaven: "*This is My beloved Son, in whom I am well-pleased*" (Matthew 3:17). He said the same thing at the transfiguration: "*This is My beloved Son, with whom I am well-pleased; listen to Him!*" (Matthew 17:5).

Besides these two occasions during the life of Jesus, the Father provided powerful testimony of the identify of Jesus in the resurrection. Paul explained to the philosophers gathered on Mars Hill: "*Because* [God] *has fixed a day in which He will judge the world in righteousness through a Man whom He has appointed, having furnished proof to all men by raising Him from the dead*" (Acts 17:31). After Jesus claimed to be equal with the Father during His life (John 5:17-18; 10:30), the fact that He was raised from the dead proved the Father's agreement with His claim. There were hundreds of witnesses that saw Jesus alive after His crucifixion (Acts 1:3; 1 Corinthians 15:3-8), confirming that this event which proved Jesus' identity as the Son of God was a historical fact.

Scripture

> "*You search the Scriptures because you think that in them you have eternal life; it is these that testify about Me; and you are unwilling to come to Me so that you may have life.*" "*Do not think that I will accuse you before the Father; the one who accuses you is Moses, in*

whom you have set your hope. For if you believed Moses, you would believe Me, for he wrote about Me. But if you do not believe his writings, how will you believe My words?" (John 5:39-40, 45-47).

The fact that the Old Testament Scriptures testified about Jesus was the basis for Paul's statement in his letter to the Galatians: *"Therefore the Law has become our tutor to lead us to Christ, so that we may be justified by faith"* (Galatians 3:24). One of the ways in which the Old Testament pointed to Jesus was through the prophecies that were made about Him. Several of these were pointed out by Matthew in his gospel:

- Jesus would be born of a virgin (Matthew 1:22-23; cf. Isaiah 7:14; 9:6-7).
- Jesus would come out of Egypt (Matthew 2:15; cf. Hosea 11:1).
- Jesus would heal the sick and cast out demons (Matthew 8:16-17; cf. Isaiah 53:4).
- Jesus would speak in parables (Matthew 13:34-35; cf. Psalm 78:2).
- Jesus would ride into Jerusalem on a donkey (Matthew 21:1-5; cf. Zechariah 9:9).
- Jesus' arrest and eventual crucifixion was done to fulfill various prophecies about Him (Matthew 26:55-56) – He would be given wine mixed with gall (Matthew 27:34; cf. Psalm 69:21); they would divide His garments and cast lots for them (Matthew 27:35; cf. Psalm 22:18); those who witnessed His crucifixion would speak against Him (Matthew 27:39; cf. Psalm 22:7). He even quoted

the words at the beginning of Psalm 22 while He hung on the cross (Matthew 27:46; cf. Psalm 22:1), pointing people back to that psalm and the prophecies it contained which were unfolding in His death.

This is not an exhaustive list; but these prophecies given in the Old Testament were fulfilled, proving that Jesus was the Son of God.

Conclusion

If Jesus simply claimed to be the Son of God, we would have no reason to believe Him. After all, others would make this same claim about themselves (cf. Matthew 24:23-24). Yet the fact that John the Baptist, the miracles Jesus performed, God the Father, and the Old Testament Scriptures all confirmed His claim shows that we can safely believe in Him today as the Christ and our Lord and Savior.

What Was Said About Jesus on the Cross?

Jesus' death on the cross is the central event of the Bible. It is the sacrifice that made forgiveness, redemption, and salvation possible for all mankind. Jesus foretold of His death (Matthew 16:21). The Scriptures prophesied of this event (Psalm 22; Isaiah 53; *et al.*). Sufficient evidence has been provided to produce belief.

In addition to all the divinely given evidence, the gospel writers also recorded comments from some uninspired men as they spoke about Jesus and His crucifixion. It is interesting to see what others understood about Him, even some without the benefit of Old Testament teaching.

Pilate – Pilate was the Roman governor over the region that included the city of Jerusalem. The Jewish leaders brought Jesus before him, intending to have Him put to death. Pilate initially resisted, but later consented after the crowd went into an uproar. When Jesus was crucified, Pilate had an inscription placed on the cross: "*Jesus the Nazarene, the King of the Jews*" (John 19:19). We do not know Pilate's motive for writing this. It is doubtful that he really believed in Jesus since he was allowing His death. But it is significant that he clearly identified who was being crucified. It was Jesus – not just any Jesus, but Jesus of Nazareth. Lest there be any further confusion, he stated that He was the one who claimed to be a king (cf. John 18:36). There would be no mistake by anyone who passed by and saw that scene. They would know who was on that cross.

The Jewish Leaders – In responding to Pilate's inscription, the Jews protested: *"Do not write, 'The King of the Jews'; but that He said, 'I am King of the Jews'"* (John 19:21). They did not want Jesus identified as their king. They told Pilate they had *"no king but Caesar"* (John 19:15). But what they did in their statement of protest was verify the claim of Jesus. They affirmed to Pilate that Jesus said He was a king. They understood Jesus' teaching. They knew His intentions. They just did not believe Him.

The Thief on the Cross – When Jesus was crucified, two thieves were crucified with Him. Luke recorded one thief challenging Jesus to save Himself and them as well. The other thief rebuked him: *"We indeed are suffering justly, for we are receiving what we deserve for our deeds; but this man has done nothing wrong." He then said to Jesus, "Remember me when You come in Your kingdom!"* (Luke 23:39-42). This thief recognized two things. First, he knew Jesus was innocent. Second, he believed that Jesus would rule over His kingdom despite certain death on the cross. Therefore, we know that Jesus was recognized as a righteous man and that His teaching about the coming kingdom was understood by certain individuals.

The Centurion – The Roman soldiers were accustomed to crucifying prisoners. It was something they were trained to do and there was usually nothing particularly unique about a crucifixion. However, this time was different. While Jesus suffered on the cross, there was darkness from the sixth hour to the ninth hour (Matthew 27:45). Immediately after His death there was an earthquake, the veil of the temple was torn in two, and the graves were opened and the dead came into the city (Matthew 27:50-53). The centurion who was there to oversee everything took note of all that happened – including all that Jesus said and did – and reached a conclusion: *"Truly this was the Son of God"* (Matthew 27:54). Did the centurion mean that he thought that Jesus was the Son of God as we understand it or just that he was righteous as Luke suggested (Luke 23:47)? In either case, this man understood that Jesus was different, was innocent, and that the power of God was with Him.

When we consider all of these things, we get an idea of what the people thought about Jesus. They recognized Him as a Jew from Nazareth. They also understood His claims of being a king. If they were honest, they recognized that there was no just cause for His condemnation. It was also plainly demonstrated that God was with Him. Besides the testimony of these uninspired men that has been recorded for us, these points are taught by the Scriptures as well. We must believe what it says, believe in Jesus, and look to Him for our salvation.

A Personal Relationship with Jesus

Many people in the religious world talk about having a "personal relationship with Jesus." On the surface, this may sound good and appealing. After all, is there anyone who believes in Jesus but would *not* want this?

However, rather than thinking about how this *sounds*, we ought to consider what this *means*. In fact, different people may mean different things when they talk about a "personal relationship with Jesus." Rather than focusing on what people might mean by this, we need to be concerned with what the Bible says. Are we to have a "personal relationship with Jesus"? If so, what is this relationship to look like? This is what we will consider in this article.

Not Biblical Language

This should be a "red flag" for us. Nowhere does the Bible talk about having a "personal relationship with Jesus." Of course, the absence of a particular *phrase* does not always mean that the *concept* described by the phrase is wrong; but we do need to be sure we understand what we are talking about. Before deciding if the phrase is acceptable or not, we need to understand what the Bible teaches. Many people who use this terminology have an incorrect idea about our relationship with Jesus.

The Relationship Described

The New Testament contains several ways in which Jesus' relationships are described. Most importantly, He was *"declared the Son of God with power by the resurrection from the dead"* (Romans 1:4). While on earth, the *"fullness of Deity"* dwelled in Him (Colossians 2:9). It is vital that we believe that Jesus is the Son of God.

There are also several ways in which Jesus' relationship with *us* – either Christians specifically or mankind generally – is described.

- Jesus is our *brother* – *"For both He who sanctifies and those who are sanctified are all from one Father; for which reason He is not ashamed to call them **brethren**"* (Hebrews 2:11). As Jesus is the *"Son of God"* (Romans 1:4), it is possible for us (Christians) to be His *"brethren"* because we are *"children of God"* through Him (1 John 3:1).
- Jesus is our *Lord* – *"Therefore let all the house of Israel know for certain that God has made Him both **Lord** and Christ—this Jesus whom you crucified"* (Acts 2:36). Being *"Lord"* means He has authority. He has the right to command us and expect us to obey Him.

- Jesus is our *Savior* – "*We have seen and testify that the Father has sent the Son to be the **Savior** of the world*" (1 John 4:14). He has made "*eternal life*" available to us so that we can avoid receiving "*the wages of sin*" (Romans 6:23).
- Jesus is our *King* – "*Jesus answered, 'My kingdom is not of this world. If My kingdom were of this world, then My servants would be fighting so that I would not be handed over to the Jews; but as it is, My kingdom is not of this realm.' Therefore Pilate said to Him, 'So You are a king?' Jesus answered, 'You say correctly that I am a **king**. For this I have been born, and for this I have come into the world, to testify to the truth. Everyone who is of the truth hears My voice*'" (John 18:36-37). As king, Jesus is the supreme ruler over His kingdom.
- Jesus is our *Judge* – "*There is only one Lawgiver and **Judge**, the One who is able to save and to destroy; but who are you who judge your neighbor?*" (James 4:12). Paul told the philosophers on Mars Hill: "*Because He has fixed a day in which He will judge the world in righteousness through a Man whom He has appointed, having furnished proof to all men by raising Him from the dead*" (Acts 17:31). He is the one who determines whether or not we are or have been faithful.

This Must Be Personal

Our relationship with Jesus is "personal" by virtue of the fact that it pertains to us as *individuals*.

- Each one of us has the opportunity to become a child of God – We can become *"sons of God through faith"* and be *"baptized into Christ"* regardless of our background (Galatians 3:26-29). Jesus commissioned His apostles: *"Go into all the world and preach the gospel to all creation. He who has believed and has been baptized shall be saved; but he who has disbelieved shall be condemned"* (Mark 16:15-16). This is open to each one of us.
- Each one of us has the ability to choose to submit to the authority of Christ – Because Jesus possesses *"all authority,"* we are to become His *"disciples"* and *"observe all that* [He] *commanded"* (Matthew 28:18-20). Paul told the brethren in Colossae, *"Whatever you do in word or deed, do all in the name of the Lord Jesus"* (Colossians 3:17). Each one of us can choose whether we will submit to Christ and obey Him or not.
- Each one of us has the potential to be saved by the Lord – Paul wrote, *"For the grace of God has appeared, bringing salvation to all men"* (Titus 2:11). Jesus' sacrifice on the cross was for *"the world"* (John 3:16). No matter who we are, each one of us has the gift of salvation available to us.
- Each one of us has the chance to be part of the kingdom – In prophesying of the establishment of the Lord's kingdom, Isaiah said, *"All the nations will stream to it"* (Isaiah 2:2). Peter explained to the household of Cornelius (a Gentile) that the kingdom was not open only to the Jews, but to all men: *"I most certainly understand now that God is not one to show partiality, but in every nation the*

man who fears Him and does what is right is welcome to Him" (Acts 10:34-35). If we will fear and obey the Lord, we can also be part of Christ's kingdom.
- Each one of us will stand before the judgment seat of Christ – Paul wrote, *"For we must all appear before the judgment seat of Christ, so that each one may be recompensed for his deeds in the body, according to what he has done, whether good or bad"* (2 Corinthians 5:10). We will each be rewarded or punished based upon how we have taken advantage of these opportunities presented to us to become children of God, to submit to the Lord, to be saved by Him, and to become part of His kingdom.

No one can do any of these things for us; therefore, any "relationship" we have with Christ will be "personal."

What This Does NOT Mean

Considering the points above about how the New Testament describes our relationship with Jesus as being "personal," we saw that this was about the fact that we have a responsibility *as individuals* to have a right relationship with Christ. Yet many come to erroneous conclusions about this. Though our relationship with Jesus must be "personal," there are some things that this does *not* mean.

- It does *not* mean that there is a different standard for each person – Paul explained to the brethren in Corinth that what he wrote constituted *"the Lord's commandment*" (1 Corinthians 14:37). The things that he taught them were the same things he taught "*everywhere in every church*" (1 Corinthians 4:17). In other words, the standard of right and wrong did not change from place to place, church to church, or person to person. We must follow the same standard the Lord has given to all men. Earlier in this letter to Corinth, Paul exhorted them to "*agree*" and be of "*the same mind and in the same judgment*" (1 Corinthians 1:10). He told the brethren in Philippi, "*Let us keep living by the same standard to which we have attained*" (Philippians 3:16).

- It does *not* mean that we are free to offer whatever service/worship is most meaningful to *us* – When Cain and Abel offered sacrifices to God, Cain, as a "*tiller of the ground*," offered a sacrifice "*of the fruit of the ground*" (Genesis 4:2-3). Many would reason that his offering should have been accepted since it was a more *personal* expression of worship than if he had offered another sacrifice (a lamb) to which he had no personal connection. However, our worship and service are for God. He wants us to "*worship in spirit and truth*" (John 4:24), not worship in whatever way is most meaningful to us. We are to "*present* [*our*] *bodies a living and holy sacrifice, acceptable to God*" (Romans 12:1) – according to His will rather than our own.

- It does *not* mean that the local church is unimportant – The church is "*the household of God*," "*the church of the living God*," and "*the pillar and support of the truth*" (1 Timothy 3:15). Therefore, the church – and the context indicates that this is the local church – is important. Many people reject "organized religion" in favor of what they claim to be a "personal relationship with Jesus." However, religion being "organized" is not the problem if it is organized according to God's will as it is revealed in His word. The problem is *man-made religion* which, as Jesus said, causes our worship to be *"in vain"* (Matthew 15:9).

According to the New Testament, our "personal relationship with Jesus" is about each of us individually making sure we are right with Christ. It is about being able to rightly call Him our *brother*, *Lord*, *Savior*, and *King*.

How We Enter into This Relationship

If we want to be able to call Jesus our *brother*, *Lord*, *Savior*, and *King*, we need to be sure we know how to enter into this relationship with Him.

- We are able to call Jesus "brother" by becoming sons of God through faith – This is not *"faith alone"* (James 2:24); rather, it is an obedient faith. We become *"sons of God through faith"* as we are *"baptized into Christ"* (Galatians 3:26-27).
- We are able to call Jesus "Lord" by doing what He says – Jesus asked, *"Why do you call Me, 'Lord, Lord,' and do not do what I say?"* (Luke 6:46). If we are not obeying Him, we cannot rightly refer to Him as our Lord. We must do the will of God

rather than doing other works while claiming they are "*in* [His] *name*" (Matthew 7:21-23).
- We are able to call Jesus "Savior" by conforming to His death, burial, and resurrection – Paul explained this in his letter to Rome: "*Or do you not know that all of us who have been baptized into Christ Jesus have been baptized into His death? Therefore we have been buried with Him through baptism into death, so that as Christ was raised from the dead through the glory of the Father, so we too might walk in newness of life. For if we have become united with Him in the likeness of His death, certainly we shall also be in the likeness of His resurrection*" (Romans 6:3-5). We can be "*reconciled to God through the death of His Son*" (Romans 5:10), but only if we conform to His death, burial, and resurrection by dying to sin, being baptized into Christ, and living as a new creature in Him.
- We are able to call Jesus "King" by being added to His kingdom, the church – Jesus explained that the *church* is the *kingdom* when He used the terms interchangeably (Matthew 16:18-19). On the day of Pentecost, God began "*adding to their number [the church, KJV] day by day those who were being saved*" (Acts 2:47). The ones who were being added were those who "*received* [Peter's] *word* [and] *were baptized*" (Acts 2:41) as he had instructed them, "*Repent, and each of you be baptized in the name of Jesus Christ for the forgiveness of your sins; and you will receive the gift of the Holy Spirit*" (Acts 2:38).

Conclusion

Jesus told the brethren in Laodicea, "*Behold, I stand at the door and knock; if anyone hears My voice and opens the door, I will come in to him and will dine with him, and he with Me*" (Revelation 3:20). He does the same for us, but we must make the decision to open the door for Him.

Will you accept Jesus as your Lord, Savior, and King? Not just in name only, but by obeying Him?

If you want to have fellowship with Christ now and in eternity, you need to faithfully follow Him. Jesus said, "*You are My friends if you do what I command you*" (John 15:14). He also said, "*If you love Me, you will keep My commandments*" (John 14:15). Are you willing to have this type of relationship with Him?

Made in the USA
Columbia, SC
19 March 2025